Tarmac Tales

By Wendy and Dave Laing

Writers Exchange E-Publishing

http://www.writers-exchange.com

Tarmac Tales

Copyright 2016 Wendy and Dave Laing
Writers Exchange E-Publishing
PO Box 372
ATHERTON QLD 4883

Cover Art by: Jatin

Published by Writers Exchange E-Publishing
http://www.writers-exchange.com

The unauthorized reproduction or distribution of this copyrighted work is illegal. Criminal copyright infringement, including infringement without monetary gain, is investigated by the FBI and is punishable by up to 5 (five) years in federal prison and a fine of $250,000.

Names, characters and incidents depicted in this book are products of the author's imagination and are used fictitiously. Any resemblance to actual events, locales, organizations, or persons, living or dead, is entirely coincidental and beyond the intent of the author.

No part of this book may be reproduced or transmitted in any form or any means, electronic or mechanical, including photocopying, recording, or by any information storage and retrieval system, without permission from the publisher.

Forward

Between us, we have a total of 52 years' experience with Airlines, in Passenger, Cargo, and dealing with Cargo Agents, Passenger Agents, Crew, Catering, and all the less obvious elements that make up the Airline Industry. We have changed names of the characters involved to keep their anonymity.

All the tales are based on fact! People who know us personally will know the names of the airlines for which we worked. We know you will enjoy reading the funny "Tarmac Tales" as much as we enjoyed collecting and collating them for you. Enjoy your behind the scenes peep!

Wendy & Dave Laing

Early Days

Wendy was born in Essendon, not far from the original Melbourne Airport, now called Essendon Fields, which still has an aviation industry operating out of the old runways.

In her childhood days, in the late 40s to early 50s, passenger planes were still propeller jobs! One of her favourite things was to hear the engineers revving up and testing the engines late at night, as she lay in bed. The sounds rattled across the empty paddocks in the still night air, creating a comforting, mesmerizing drone, which helped her to get to sleep.

Little did she know that many years later, she would be involved in the industry herself.

Dave, as a child, lived on a farm near the Royal Airforce Base at Leuchars, in Fife, Scotland.

Again in the late 40s and 50s, there were the old prop aircraft movements, followed later by the Vulcan Bombers flying overhead when Dave was playing or working in the fields below.

Little did he know that he was going to spend thirty-two years in this exciting industry.

It was this industry that brought Wendy and Dave together!

In 1962, Wendy's school had a week's excursion to Tasmania, flying out of Essendon Airport to Hobart. The group was divided onto two separate flights. Wendy was one of the volunteers to go on the old DC3, whilst the rest of the group went on the newer Fokker friendship, which departed half an hour later.

It was a fun flight for Wendy, as it flew at a low altitude, and bumped through the clouds over the mountains in Tasmania. A few of the other girls were rather green by the time the aircraft arrived at Hobart. To everyone's amazement, the rest of the group, who had flown out half an hour later from Melbourne, were already standing at the fence in Hobart waving a greeting.

Such was the difference in the speed of the older prop aircraft versus the more modern aircraft that the other half of the group had flown on!

Dave's first commercial flight was in 1963 on a Viscount aircraft from Heathrow to Edinburgh. He bought a standby ticket for two pounds and was lucky to get one of the last seats.

The unfortunate thing, when he landed in Edinburgh, was that the airline had misplaced his baggage.

The baggage finally arrived the next day and was delivered to his home in Fife in a damaged condition. He put in a claim for the damage and received back the princely sum of seven shillings!

Wendy's first international flight was out of the then new Tullamarine Airport, on a Boeing 707 to Honolulu via Sydney.

It was during the first few months' operation of the airport. Everything was sparkling new.

It was certainly a new experience for Wendy, as she was quite used to flying domestically on only the older prop aircraft and the newer small jet aircraft. The 707 seemed enormous to her at that time.

Taking off from Sydney was a fantastic experience; flying out over the Sydney Harbour Heads and over the Pacific enjoying the longevity of the flight, the meals, and of course, the movies, which were screened onto the large screen located on the bulkhead at the front of each cabin section.

Just as well Wendy had an aisle seat to see the movie, because of certain heads blocking the view! Also, the movie was screened at a certain time, and there was basically no choice of what was screened.

On hindsight, the aircraft was so small, compared to the new A380s which have all the benefits of individual entertainment kits with music, games and a huge choice of movies available.

Back in the mid 60s, when Dave was in the British Territorial Army, he did a few flights on RAF Britannia aircraft, where the passengers always sat backwards for safety reasons.

The cargo and baggage was stowed between the cockpit and the passenger section.

On one particular flight, from Sharjah (Trucial States, now known as UAE) via Limassol (Cyprus) to Lyneham in England, he was first on board the aircraft, and so had the cargo at the back of his seat.

For the whole flight, he could not put his seat back. He was also suffering from sunburn, which he'd gained from the hot desert sun. As a result, he had to lean forward in his seat to stop the pain from the blisters on his back.

Wow, what a terrible flight!

Aircraft Adventures

Many years ago, Dave was travelling around New Zealand and visited *The Hermitage* at Mount Cook.

The weather was bright and sunny, so Dave decided to go on a ski plane flight to the top of the Tasman Glacier. The ski plane had wheels plus skis for landing on snow or ice.

What an experience it was to land on pure ice on the aircraft's skis! The passengers all climbed out of the plane and gingerly walked around on the slippery ice in beautiful sunshine high in the mountains.

After reboarding the light aircraft, the Captain took off towards the snow covered, steep face of Mount Cook.

Dave was lucky to be sitting up front in the co-pilot's seat. The pilot took the aircraft as close as he could near the side of the mountain, and then veered off at the last second.

Wow, that was scary! By the time everyone got their breath back, the pilot was heading back to *The Hermitage* where he landed the plane, just like a normal aircraft on wheels on the tarmac. The journey was then almost like a dream, and a hair raising one at that!

In the late 1960s, Wendy was staying at the family holiday house at Mornington, on Port Phillip Bay.

After shopping with her father, late in the morning to get some food essentials for her mother, she noticed a small helicopter flying overhead at a low altitude, heading towards the Park on the bluff near the pier.

Naturally, Wendy and her father headed down to the park to investigate. The Ansett helicopter was taking joy rides around the district to raise money for charity. The flights were for a maximum of two passengers in the little Bell Helicopter, and were for a fifteen minute ride.

Of course, they couldn't resist, and lined up.

Their turn came after nearly an hour. They climbed aboard and buckled themselves in. Wendy's father had his camera with him (as usual) and got ready to take snaps of the adventure.

The Captain asked if they had anywhere special nearby that they wished to fly over.

"Of course," said Wendy's dad. "We have a house on Beleura Hill over there," pointing to the second bluff away.

Off they flew, eyes bulging with excitement. Once the chopper got to Beleura Hill, the house was pointed out to the pilot, who grinned and said, "Hey someone's sunbathing on the sundeck. Get your camera ready, Peter, and I'll go down and hover over the house for you to take a snap."

Despite hovering, tilting the chopper, yelling out of the open doors and waving, no one stirred in the house, or moved on the sundeck!

The flight ended up taking over twenty minutes, but was well worth every second.

When Wendy and her father arrived back to the house, they drove down into the carport. Her mother was the first to open the front door.

"Where have you two been? You missed a helicopter flying overhead, making a huge noise--what a stupid pilot!"

There was laughter, when they told the family who the two passengers were and that no-one moved on the sundeck or waved back!

One spooky note to this tale--several years later a bell helicopter crashed at Essendon Airport when coming into land. The only person on board was the pilot--the same one who had flown them that day years earlier!

During Dave's visit to Sharjah when in the British Territorial Army in the 60s, part of the training was in an old Wessex helicopter.

Dave was seated against the wall opposite the main door. Everyone had their 40 pound packs on their backs, which made it difficult to sit back properly in the seat. They were all strapped in with a lap belt only.

On take-off, the pilot headed for the nearby desert. Once there, the sergeant yelled in his booming voice, what was going to happen next.

The helicopter was now hovering. It then tilted to the left at about 45 degrees, meaning that Dave was looking at the horizon and blue sky. The chopper was then moved back to a horizontal hover, and then tilted 45 degrees to the right. Dave, clutching his rifle, was now looking out at the sand, fifty feet below, and praying that his safety belt would hold!

At last, after what seemed like an eternity, the pilot straightened up the chopper while Dave's mates all laughed at the look of frozen fear etched on his face.

On return to base, Dave's jelly legs stepped down onto the tarmac with some relief!

Quote: Airlink was the brand name of a helicopter shuttle service which ran between London's two main airports, Gatwick and Heathrow, between 1978 and 1986. Operated jointly by British Caledonian Airways and British Airways Helicopters using a Sikorsky S-61 owned by the British Airports Authority, the "curious and unique operation" connected the rapidly growing airports in the years before the M25 motorway existed. Although at one point the service was granted a licence to operate until 1994, the Secretary of State for Transport intervened and revoked the licence with effect from February 1986--by which time the continued existence of the link had become a "highly controversial issue" debated by Members of Parliament, airlines, airport operators, local authorities and many other interest groups. No similar service has operated between the airports since Airlink's cessation. End quote. (http://en.wikipedia.org/wiki/Airlink (helicopter shuttle service).

Wendy actually travelled from Heathrow to Gatwick on this service back in 1979.

What a unique experience! Once on-board, the captain and co-pilot ensured everyone was belted into their seats. The engine started and the walls inside shook in time to the 'throb--throb--throb' noise outside.

On take-off, the big helicopter slowly rose gracefully into the air, turned, and then headed across land for the 30 mile trip to Gatwick. The flight was only 15 minutes. What a difference to going by taxi via the old road network of the day!

On hind sight, such a service would be a nice 'romantic' ride between these airports, instead of using the M25, which today is clogged with traffic.

Back in the early 70s, Dave decided to have a holiday in the Bahamas and Florida.

One of his many highlights of the trip was a Cessna flight from Fort Lauderdale Airport to Key West. Again, he happened to be lucky to sit in the co-pilot's seat for the hour long journey.

What a tremendous view of the long state road over the Keys and the bridges to Key West!

After landing at Key West, he booked a coach trip around the township, visiting the home of Earnest Hemmingway and the Port area, and seeing a sign pointing out to sea, "Cuba 90 miles". Key West was a lovely town. It was like going into a time warp of the 1930s.

On the flight back from Key West to Fort Lauderdale, a big storm followed them all the way. Behind them, Dave could see this huge front of black storm cloud. Luckily they made it back to Fort Lauderdale just in time. Five minutes after landing, this tropical rain storm hit with a vengeance when everyone was in the safety of the terminal.

In the mid-70s, when Wendy was holidaying in Hawaii, she went on a Beechcraft day trip around the Hawaiian Islands.

She had to be up with the larks, as the bus picked her up from the hotel at 5.30 am, and took her to the back of the Honolulu airport to a hanger. Here, she met the other passengers over a light breakfast of croissants and coffee before take-off.

The first leg went from Honolulu to Maui, and was an idyllic experience, flying across the deep blue waters of the Pacific.

The day trip included stopovers on Maui, with a short bus tour, then around the coast of the big Island of Hawaii and its huge crater, and finally Kauai, with a visit to the famous Fern Grotto. The trip returned to Honolulu airport at dusk.

Strangely enough, Dave did the same tour about the same time. He was lucky to be sitting in the co-pilot seat for the whole trip.

In 1984, when Wendy and Dave were honeymooning in Maui, they realised that they had both done the same island day trip in the same year, but never met!

In 2005, Wendy & Dave travelled via the famous Ghan from Adelaide to Darwin and back.

Whilst the train stopped in Katherine, Northern Territory, passengers could indulge in a scenic helicopter ride around the area for 5 minutes.

Luckily, Wendy & Dave got the last trip for the day, and the pilot asked if they wanted a slightly longer trip to see the train from the air.

"Of course" was the response.

The little Bell helicopter took off and headed to the railway line. The wind was very strong and gusty that day, and the chopper had no doors, so the wind blew through the cabin. Dave, as usual sat next to the pilot, because he had his video camera. The pilot obliged by doing two extra runs over the train and the video results were fantastic!

Some of the train passengers were a little jealous when told about the flight over the train. Most of them had been too scared to fly.

Airline Alliances

We would like to point out here, that in the days we worked at Tullamarine together on the tarmac, and also during Wendy's days working in the city ticket office, there were many, many times when we socialised with the 'opposition' and also helped each other in time of need.

We have decided to include some of these moments into our Tarmac Tales.

Airlines swapped equipment or 'borrowed' cargo pallets, containers, or tie-down restrainers, when needed urgently. If another airline had some spare pallets, one only needed to ask.

Everyone basically worked hard for their respective airlines, but when it came to 'after hours' all enjoyed socialising together.

These interline friendships formed a larger 'family' who became firm friends outside the industry, even after retirement.

We'll start with a very sad occasion. Wendy had changed to a different airline at the airport, but was still, at that time, working in the same Airline Cargo Handling Agent's building, on the same floor.

She had arrived early to work that day, and immediately sensed a gloomy atmosphere as she entered the front office of the building. The handling staff called her over.

"Did you hear the news this morning?"

"No, not yet, why?"

"Your old airline's aircraft... the one that left Melbourne yesterday... there was a terrible accident... I'm sorry..."

Wendy was in a state of shock. She had been talking to that crew on the tarmac the morning they left, as obviously she knew them from the years she worked with them. The Captain was a Senior Captain, who flew for the US Airforce reserve when on leave. The first officer, flight engineer, and maintenance engineer were very experienced.

Apparently the weather was very bad at the time, very low visibility, and one of the radars at Kuala Lumpur control was down.

For those of you who have landed there, you will appreciate the rugged, mountainous territory on approach to the airport.

Wendy went upstairs to her airline office, and was immediately offered a coffee and condolences. It was one very flat day, with every other airline at the airport offering their help and support. No staff liked to hear of accidents involving fellow airlines.

One time, when working in the Melbourne ticket office, Wendy was asked by a passenger for an urgent ticket rewrite.

The passenger asked if there were two seats on the flight to London that night. There were. She booked their seats. It was a compassionate case, as the mother-in-law was suddenly seriously ill back in England. However their ticket was a 'special' restricted ticket, which was basically non-endorsable to another airline.

Wendy was a widow of British Airways, and although she now worked for the opposition, she obviously knew their staff in Melbourne.

A quick phone call produced the authority to change the ticket. She rushed around the corner to their office, and the problem was solved.

Normally, such a change could take over a day to fix, waiting for responses from the UK, involving time zone differences.

So Wendy owed British Airways a favour? No, not with such a close tie to them and their Melbourne staff.

Back in Wendy's Travel agency days, she worked in the same building as the Pan American ticket office.

Her manager came to her, and asked her if she could hand write some tickets for them downstairs for an hour or so.

Apparently their main computer at Tullamarine and city office had broken down, and two of the six staff had never learnt to manually write airline tickets, like travel agents were doing at that time.

Yes, she obliged. Years later, the same Pan American Manager 'organised' free tickets to Honolulu for Wendy & Dave's honeymoon!

Dave's company was doing the ground handling for Pan American Airways. He had to go up to their office the morning after one of their aircraft had collided with KLM at Las Palmas the day before.

The atmosphere was pure gloom. Dave was shown a telex by the staff, which said 'N734 PA (registration number) no longer in service!'

That was the only communication from New York. That aircraft had been in Melbourne the week before! All the staff with true professionalism got on with their job at hand and prepared for the day's aircraft departure.

One time, when Wendy's airline was being handled by a new agent at the airport, there was another great example of interline friendship displayed.

The new agent was positioned next door to the old agent. Dave was in fact now working next door to Wendy.

There was a full cargo load of pregnant cattle on board the aircraft on the tarmac, ready to go to Taiwan for breeding. Suddenly, the agent's main deck loader seized while loading that deck.

The loader was towed away, but the lower deck doors in the cargo hold had just been closed. They couldn't load the last pallet of cows on the main deck, and in the meantime, the lower deck cattle were now not getting air-conditioning!

The tarmac people, including people from the old handling agent, frantically reopened the lower doors. Initially, Wendy was told that that they would have to wait for over an hour for another main deck loader from Qantas. Wendy's airline normally didn't use their equipment--but within five minutes, they produced one, knowing the urgency with pregnant cows and a flight crew likely to run out of hours!

Such cooperation was always welcome in our days at Tullamarine!

Agents Angles

During her days as a ticket officer in the city office, Wendy had to deal on roster with passengers and agents. Travel agents in particular were always in a rush and always busy. One agent was renowned for trying to 'block' off extra seats during the busy Christmas season for her clients. The favourite trick or 'angle' was to make bookings on their computer using different 'common' Chinese names such as Chan, Leung, Ho and the like. Agents did not have the authority to make a name change or spelling change in their bookings. They had to come to the airline concerned to get one of the ticket officers to change the name. Of course, there had to be a valid reason, such as an obvious mistyping or misspelling of the name.

This agent came in two weeks before Christmas with a swag of bookings with names to be 'adjusted' due misspelling! The ticketing deadline was the next day and all the flights were fully booked. The agent leaned over Wendy's desk and said, "Please Wendy, I'm soooo busy, soooo rushed and I seem to have made a few spelling mistakes on these bookings." She flashed Wendy an endearing smile. "I'm sooo sorry, but could you make the name changes?" She handed Wendy a list containing over one hundred name changes! Argh! They were all showing Leung to change to Ling, Cheong to Chung etc. She even tried the scenario of "Oh and with this one, I reversed the surname with the given name!"

Wendy, backed up by her supervisor and Manager, politely asked her to rebook every booking. Incidentally, although she had to re-book every passenger and although they were all waitlisted, eventually everyone was confirmed due to the usual overbooking on every flight at that time of the year. That agent never tried that 'angle' of illegally blocking off seats with false names again!

Another travel agent was famous for always talking loudly in his native tongue on his mobile phone, as he entered the office. He would stride up to the Agency Desk and plonk down his paperwork, then wave his arm and click his fingers all the time, continuing to talk on his phone.

Wendy had tried to ask him to stop talking on the phone and communicate direct, but he ignored these requests. So it was decided that next time he came in, that staff would not serve him until he stopped chatting on his mobile and put it away and spoke politely to them. The Airline staff were determined to try and get him to be polite.

The following day, he came in and was chatting loudly on his mobile. Other travel agents were in the office at that time, waiting quietly for their tickets to be issued.

(We must explain why the agents were collecting tickets from the airline direct, here:

It was the time, that airlines were issuing 'net' tickets for the agents, as they had an agreement with the airline for 'overriding' or 'higher' commissions, than if they issued the tickets themselves via the Travel Agent's Bank Settlement Plan. This was quite a legal practice, but it meant that they had to come to the airline ticket office to receive and pay direct for their tickets to be issued. Now back to our tale about the noisy agent.)

He continued to chat on his phone, and this day, pushed to the front of the queue, aggressively tapped his finger on the desk for attention and then tapped his hand on his watch, in sign language to indicate he was in a hurry.

Suddenly the phone he was holding to his left ear rang loudly!

Everyone in the office started to laugh at him. He wasn't even talking to anyone on his phone. It was all a big pose. Scarlet-faced, he sheepishly went to the back of the queue.

When his turn came, he actually spoke to staff politely, and in turn was handled efficiently and quickly. It was a lesson well learnt!

One day, Carl, a fellow cargo agent with Dave, was serving a freight forwarder who was lodging unaccompanied baggage on behalf of a client who was travelling to Turkey.

The freight forwarder and his clients put the three heavy suitcases on the scales.

Carl continued to type up the airway bill (the days before computers) on a typewriter. On completion, he re-checked the weight of the cases and found a discrepancy of some 20 kilos.

He discovered that two of the freight forwarders clients had put their toes under the edge of the scales to lift them to get the lighter weight.

Carl was angry and pulled the airway bill out of the typewriter and wrote cancelled across the document. He then told the forwarder that he either took the baggage elsewhere or "We start again".

Eventually, the airway bill with the correct weight was completed, monies paid, and the forwarder, suitably chastened, went on his way.

Dave was working at the international passenger check-in counter, servicing one of the airlines that his company handled in cargo. His job was to take excess baggage, as unaccompanied baggage which would travel on the next available flight as cargo.

A passenger who was checking in his baggage also had a lawnmower which was full of fuel. The passenger agent immediately told the passenger that he was not permitted to take the lawnmower with him, because the fuel was classed as flammable material. After a lot of argument, his family took the lawnmower home.

Five minutes later, four men arrived with a 95 kilo trunk to check in as baggage. Again the passenger agent rejected the trunk as being too heavy, but it could be sent, if only containing personal effects, as unaccompanied baggage.

They were directed to Dave, the cargo agent at the end of the counter. Dave gave him a quote which was half the general cargo rate.

The passenger could not afford that amount of money. Argument ensued as to why he could not take it on board and eventually he decided to leave it behind.

One of the passenger agents exclaimed in a loud voice, "Heck, the next thing we'll see a kitchen sink coming in the door to put on board!"

Two minutes later, a man walked in with a kitchen sink under his arm! This caused much hilarity. On the other hand, it was rather sad that these passengers, who were returning home to central Europe, were taking things that they couldn't buy in their home villages.

Wendy was travelling home after a week's course in Hong Kong. She went to the counter, and received a big smile from the passenger check-in lady when she saw her staff ticket.

"Did you have enough time to do some shopping?"

"Of course!" replied Wendy.

"That's good. Could you put your suitcase onto the scales, and I'll then put it through the x-ray machine."

This was standard procedure at Kai Tak airport.

A few minutes later, the lady returned to the desk, looking embarrassed.

"Um. There's something suspicious showing in your case."

Wendy was suitably embarrassed. "What does it look like?"

"It looks like batteries, and a clock mechanism."

"Oops, I put my travel clock in my case, instead of in my carry-on bag!"

Unfortunately, the supervisor in charge insisted on opening the suitcase at the counter, while everyone watched. Luckily, Wendy located the travel clock quickly. She was allowed to put it in her hand baggage. Even the supervisor giggled.

"Easy thing to do, Wendy."

Wendy was glad to disappear through the customs door away from curious eyes at the counter.

Obviously Wendy was tired after a hectic week of classes that trip, as she knew all the rules of her airline.

As she arrived at the boarding gate, after her travel clock incident, she noticed that the queue was very long, and the boarding rather slow.

As she got nearer, she saw the reason why. It was common knowledge with her airline that when people checked in at the main counter, they got friends to 'hide' their large cabin bags, known in the industry as 'Asian' suitcases. This nickname was used for the excess baggage that passengers shoved in extra clothing and souvenirs that they couldn't fit in their normal 20kg suitcase, or their regulation carry-on baggage. They bought these large three feet square woven plastic bags cheaply in the markets. These bags had standard red white & blue large stripes and a zip around the edge, with two handles on the top.

Because the check-in counter hadn't seen them, and had only weighed & checked the 'normal' allowed items, the passengers thought that they could now grab the large 'Asian' suitcases and take them through to the boarding gate and on board.

Aha! Upon arrival at the boarding gate, the airline's cargo agents were standing by, and were taking the large bags, weighing them, then charging them unaccompanied baggage rates. The bags were then tagged, and the receipt chit handed to the passengers concerned, who then would have to go to the cargo office after they were notified when their bag had arrived back home.

This was often a few days later, because of the full passenger loads and heavy scheduled cargo that was on board all the flights from Hong Kong to Australia.

Passenger Personalities

The biggest problems that airline crews face are drunken passengers. Wendy still remembers vividly one such 'happy' drunk on a flight years ago when travelling to America.

She was a passenger on a DC8, now replaced by the 747 aircraft. The DC8 only had a single aisle, which ran down the centre of the passenger cabin with three seats on each side. A couple of hours out of Nandi, Fiji after a fuel stop, Wendy noticed that the crew were having a little difficulty controlling a passenger sitting in the window seat with two empty adjacent seats on the opposite side from herself. Despite advising the passenger that they could not serve him any more alcohol, the man seemed to be getting drunker as each hour of the journey progressed.

Eventually the evening meal dishes were collected and passengers were bedding down for a few hours of sleep before reaching Honolulu, Hawaii. The now happy drunk had started to sing bawdy sailing songs. Nearby passengers tried in vain to keep him quiet. One woman, seated behind, pulled the crew assist button. When the steward arrived, the woman tactfully announced that she had managed to 'sneak' away one of the two duty free whisky bottles that the man had been happily gulping from! Both bottles were confiscated for the rest of the flight.

Wendy finally dozed off and so did the drunk...when suddenly there was a loud announcement from the drunk, "Wow, I've gotta get another drink!" He put on his light, crawled over the two empty adjacent seats and promptly fell on his hands and knees into the aisle. Lights turned on around the crumpled heap, nose down, backside up, snoring loudly! The aisle was completely blocked.

It took three of the crew assisted by several passengers, including Wendy, amid fits of giggling to lift the 'dead-weight' and drag him to the back of the aircraft, where he was laid on the floor to sleep it off, out of harm's way.

One tale from a fellow airline employee is about a flight out of Delhi to London on the then new 'Hush Power' VC10 aircraft, which he was on years earlier.

The employee, Stan, was a purser on the airline. He told Wendy that prior to the flight, all the migrant passengers had been shown how to use 'western' toilets on the aircraft, in a specially designed room in the airport. These passengers had never flown before, and were migrants to England under the migrant scheme, as they held British passports. They were hoping for a better life and future for their children. Most of them had come straight from their small huts on community farms where the toilets were basically a hole in the ground, where there were no sanitary necessities.

The flight finally took off, and everything seemed to be going smoothly. The crew were serving lunch an hour after take-off, when suddenly, Stan could smell smoke coming from the back of the aircraft.

He grabbed an extinguisher from the galley and rushed down the aisle towards a couple, sitting crossed-legged in the aisle. They were huddled around a pot, with some sticks, trying to fan the sticks into flames!

Stan yelled at them, and pointed the extinguisher at them and the small camp fire in the aisle.

After telling this tale to Wendy on a flight to London years later, when he was the senior purser, he laughed and said, "It was the first time I'd seen two passengers who looked like two snowmen after I'd finished extinguishing the fire!"

Passengers, particularly when nervous, seem to talk incessantly or prattle. Wendy will always remember the time when she was the travel agent who had organised a particular group tour for the 'TV Week' Magazine. The trip was to see the Oscar Awards in Hollywood. She was enjoying a pre-trip cocktail party given by the host airline for a TV awards tour to the United States and the joys of Hollywood.

She was chatting politely to the well-known tour leader, a famous television celebrity of the time, his wife and the manager of the airline. A blue-rinsed haired elderly woman, booked on the tour, came across and introduced herself. She was from the bush and had never travelled in a plane, let alone out of the country. She appeared very anxious as she asked, "I'm worried about the fact that you've just told us that we will now be travelling in a smaller plane between Melbourne and Auckland."

The manager raised one eyebrow and responded, "Well the DC8 is still a big aircraft. What exactly are you worried about?"

"Well, because it's smaller than the plane we will be flying in from Auckland to Los Angeles...I just want to know if the smaller plane will be able to carry enough oxygen in it for us to breathe?"

Goodness knows how any of us managed to keep serious looks on our faces as we all assured her that all planes, regardless of their size, carried enough oxygen for all the passengers on board.

Not long after the first pure jet aircraft, the DC9, went into service in Australia, a big bronzed Aussie, a first time passenger, on seeing the plane on the tarmac was heard to say, "I'm not getting on that thing. It has no propellers!" With that, he waited for the next plane to his destination in an old Electra complete with four propellers!

On another occasion, several passengers queued at the check-in desk holding items, which the airline clerk immediately advised, "I'm sorry, but they will have to go in the cargo hold with your suitcases."

"But why mate? We need these stools, as we won't get seats on board because we're on standby tickets!" Brings to mind a possible cartoon showing standby passengers standing in the aisles, holding onto hand straps, just like passengers do on trams, buses and trains.

Dave was told this next story by a flight attendant from the United Kingdom who was on an aircraft carrying migrants from Prestwick (near Glasgow) to Toronto, Canada. One of the female passengers was concerned that her children were getting bored. When the flight attendant walked by, she asked, "Excuse me, can my children go out to play?"

During her travel agent days, Wendy was working for a wholesale company, planning trips for special groups and writing brochures whilst liaising with the tour leaders.

When her holidays were due, the manager of the agency asked Wendy if she would like a free trip to Hawaii.

The only catch was that she was the 'unofficial' tour leader. The particular package of seven days was based on a minimum of ten passengers, so as fifteen were travelling on that date, Wendy was given a free airline ticket plus free accommodation, as the agent's tour organiser.

Wendy thought this would be a breeze. 'Wrong!' On take-off she couldn't help but notice two very nervous indigenous young ladies, who actually seemed to turn white as the aircraft gathered speed down the runway at Melbourne.

They were sitting opposite her across the aisle, so Wendy started talking to them.

"First time on an aircraft?"

"Oooooh yes!"

Wendy knew who they were, as she had a list of the passengers of her group with her. They were from northern Victoria.

"Did you fly down to Melbourne?"

"No we came by bus, 'cause it was cheaper."

Wendy noticed the clenched fists.

"Don't worry, it's just like being in that bus, so don't worry about the bumps and shakes when we're in the air. Think of the bumps and shakes that you had in the bus to Melbourne."

The trick worked. The two girls smiled and relaxed as the plane took off.

"Whoopee, Honolulu, here we come," said the one seated next to the aisle across from Wendy.

The flight was uneventful. Nearing Honolulu, Wendy chatted again to the two young ladies, telling them about the beautiful blue waters of Waikiki beach and the fun time they were going to have.

Alas, as they came through the dark clouds, Wendy noticed rain pelting on the windows.

Upon arrival, the local handling travel agent tour leader, who was taking care of the group for the week, came across to Wendy and introduced herself.

"I hope your passengers are ready to take off their shoes to wade to the bus taking them to the hotel."

Ugh! She wasn't wrong. There had been ten inches of rain, and there was water everywhere.

"Don't worry, Wendy, the water will clear up by tomorrow morning, and the sun will be shining for the rest of the week."

With fingers crossed, Wendy and the rest of the group paddled over to the bus, which went to the hotel.

Everyone identified their bags in the lobby for them to be taken to their respective rooms.

It was only ten minutes after Wendy got to her room, ready for a good night's sleep after the long flight from home, when the phone rang.

"There's a Mr Brown wanting to talk to you. Apparently he's not happy with his room! Shall I put him through?"

Obviously Wendy had little choice. She spoke to Mr Brown, who seemed rather angry, telling her that the ceiling in his room was leaking from all the rain, and their bed was soaking wet.

Wendy knew that the hotel wasn't fully booked, so she replied, "I'll come up to look myself, and don't worry, I'll organise another room for you both."

She went up two floors. Mr Brown's description was very accurate. The bed was very wet. The roof above the hotel was flat, and obviously the water had not drained properly to the downpipes.

Wendy used Mr Brown's hotel phone and called reception.

"Mr Brown is quite correct. Their bed is not fit to sleep in. I'm quite sure that he didn't order a water bed! Could you please upgrade the Browns for the night?"

Mr Brown grinned, and then burst into laughter after Wendy hung up.

Five minutes later, Mr and Mrs Brown were ushered to a better room. Wendy had won a firm friend for the rest of the week. The next morning, the rest of the group were leaving for a flight to the island of Hawaii for two nights, and Wendy was then able to relax for her own holiday.

When she went down to the lobby, there was Mr Brown, organising the correct name labels on the bags for the bus which was taking them to the airport.

He whispered to Wendy, "Have a lovely holiday. We'll see you in a week. The local agent told me that you are not the official tour leader, but it's your company's brochure, and it was you who actually set up this tour for them!"

Just proves, a little customer service goes a long way!

Dave was flying from JFK, New York to Heathrow London back in the 1970s.

As he was boarding the aircraft, he was asked to put his cabin bag through the x-ray machine. As he continued through the security frame, a voice called, "Whose bag is this!" He was pointing to Dave's bag.

"It's mine," replied Dave.

"Would you mind stepping this way, sir?" The security guard picked up Dave's bag and took him into a room at the side.

Dave suddenly realised that he was in this room with the security personnel and two burley New York policemen with their hands on their pistols!

"Would you mind opening this bag, sir, and empty it on the table?"

Nervously, Dave unzipped the bag and took the contents out. At the bottom of the bag, he had a camera tripod in a leather zip case. Security asked him, "What's in that little case, sir?"

Dave explained it was a tripod for his camera. On seeing the tripod, there were sighs and laughter all around, as the agent explained that it had shown on the x-ray like a rifle butt!

Apologies were given and accepted as Dave repacked his bag and everyone shook hands. Dave continued on his flight.

When Wendy and Dave were honeymooning in the islands of Hawaii, they were flying from Honolulu to Maui for a week at the Hyatt Regency resort.

There were no seat allocations on the domestic flights within the island group. It was only a short twenty minute flight and it was economy only. There was a large group of Japanese honeymooners on the same flight, who all made a dash for the seats at the front.

Wendy & Dave struggled down the aisle to finally find two seats, just over the wings. They were the last two passengers on board.

The cabin door closed, and the aircraft started to taxi out to the runway. A steward approached Wendy and Dave and asked them if they could please moved down to the last two seats in the tail of the aircraft. He said that none of the Japanese group wanted to move.

Wendy and Dave both asked, "Why?"

"To help trim the aircraft!"

Wendy and Dave both replied that two people weren't going to make much of a difference, and it was a bit late, as the aircraft was about to take off! The engines started to roar.

There was no time for anyone to move. The steward promptly sat down and strapped himself in, in the seat behind them.

Amazingly, the aircraft took off without any incident. One could say that that aircraft took off rather nose-heavy that day!

One flight that Wendy came home from Hong Kong on, after a week's course, was fully booked.

She was lucky to get an aisle seat in the third section down the back of the aircraft. It was late at night, and Wendy realised that she was in for a flight where it might be difficult to sleep.

After a light supper was served, Wendy settled down for some sleep. The cabin lights were quickly dimmed.

The two passengers seated next to Wendy were Chinese who didn't speak any English. They appeared to be father and son. The son was a very big boy!

A couple of hours later, Wendy finally dosed off. She woke up about an hour later finding it hard to breathe. Something was lying on top of her! That something was the large boy, who had his feet lying across his father, who was snoring loudly. The boy's body was across his seat, with both armrests up. His head and shoulders were lying across Wendy!

Wendy managed to press her call button. The purser came down the aisle and gasped!

He immediately tapped the sleeping lump on top of her and shook him awake. He spoke to the father and son in Mandarin. His voice was low, but threatening. He kept pointing at Wendy, smiling at her.

Finally, the father nodded, and the son sat up in his seat, with the arms down--seat inclined back, ready to sleep.

The purser whispered in English to Wendy, "I'm so sorry, Wendy. I know you are staff. I'd like to offer you a spare seat, but there are none. However, if you'd like to come down to the galley and crew rest area for a drink for a while, we can keep an eye on that young man and make sure he's properly asleep, in his own seat, before you settle down."

Wendy accepted the offer and was given some first class service down the back galley, with a glass of whisky and some hot nibbles for the next hour.

Finally, she went back to her seat and smiled. The purser smiled back, "Have a good sleep for what's left of the flight, Wendy."

She did. Mind you, the whisky helped!

On a wintery night flight, during the mid-1970s, Dave flew from Vancouver to Toronto with a stopover in Edmonton.

Before take-off from Edmonton, the ground crews had to put hot air blowers on all the doors and wings to de-ice them before the DC8 could depart.

The temperature in the cabin rose quite considerably and all the passengers started taking off their jackets and pullovers.

This was a common occurrence for the local travellers, but for Dave, it was a new experience.

On the last night of Wendy's Honolulu free holiday for her Travel Agency, using a tour leader's ticket, she was wondering how her group enjoyed their week's holiday around the Hawaiian Islands.

She would know the next morning, when they arrived back at her Honolulu hotel for one night's stay before she joined the whole group for the long flight back to Melbourne.

She was walking to the elevator to go back up to her room, when a familiar voice called out to her.

"Wendy! Fancy seeing you here!"

Wendy instantly recognised a former workmate from another travel agency where she had worked a couple of years earlier.

They went for a quiet drink in the bar to catch up with each other.

Wendy explained that she was an 'unofficial' tour leader.

"Well, Wendy, would you believe I've just had two weeks in California with a group, as an official tour leader. First time for me too." She paused, and laughed. "What a disaster! Well, the beginning of it was anyway."

Janet then told Wendy her Passenger Personality experience.

One of her passengers, a single man in his twenties, had left with her from Melbourne and travelled via Auckland to Los Angeles. Apparently during the last leg of the flight, nearing Honolulu, Fred was looking nervous and restless. The cabin crew alerted her, and she spent the last hour sitting next to him. Her friendly chatter seemed to calm him down.

Everything went smoothly during the landing, going through customs, and the bus to the hotel in downtown Hollywood.

Janet finally got everyone settled into their rooms, and then went to her own.

An hour later, the desk clerk called her room.

"Janet, we have the police here. They want you to go with them to identify a gentleman called Fred who says he's a member of your tour group."

Janet pulled on her clothes, and went down to the lobby and joined the two burly Los Angeles policemen.

Upon arriving at the local police station, Janet was taken to a room where Fred was sitting in a suspect's zippered outfit. Janet immediately wondered what he'd done.

The Sergeant explained. "Ma'am, we found Fred here running down Sunset Boulevard without a stitch on!"

Janet saw the funny side, then realised that Fred was again very restless and sounding incoherent.

She told the police that she had a list of contacts for each of her group. She looked up Fred's contact, who was his brother in Melbourne. She rang his number.

"What's up?" asked Fred's brother.

Janet then told him where Fred was, and that he was facing charges of indecency in a public place.

To her horror, the brother was quite calm.

"Oh, I'm not surprised. He only got out of a mental rehab hospital a couple of days ago! I got him his passport and booked his trip. He really wanted to go, and the doctors said that as long as he took his medications, he'd be fine!"

Janet shook her head.

"I'll pass you over to the Sergeant, and he'll tell you what is going to happen. I'll have to step back now, as he's now no longer under my supervision."

Janet then told Wendy that Fred was now in a mental rehab hospital in Los Angeles, and when he was finally released, he would have to be deported to Melbourne under medical supervision.

Janet was fairly calm about the episode, as her husband was an eminent psychiatrist in Melbourne.

"I phoned my hubby, and he was able to liaise with someone he knew at the facility in Melbourne where Fred had been. He reckoned that we were lucky that Fred hadn't done something weird on the aircraft."

Just goes to show, that having a passport doesn't guarantee the physical or mental health of a passenger!

Talking about nervous passengers reminds Wendy of her own experience whilst flying from Melbourne to Auckland.

The flight was on Good Friday, and Wendy and her first late husband were 'hitching' a free ride on his airline. They went to Auckland each Easter for a few days to visit his sister and family.

Approaching Auckland, the weather had deteriorated, and the 747 Captain advised that there were cross winds on landing and to expect a little turbulence on approach.

Having landed at Auckland many times, Wendy was a little tense, as there is only one runway from East to West, so the southerly strong winds weren't inviting.

Sitting in first class, on the left in a window seat, Wendy looked out at the familiar approach across the sea. The clouds were thick and the sea disappeared from view as the side wind battered the large aircraft.

The plane came out of the clouds, which were very low. Just as the runway appeared on her left, Wendy felt a strong gust from the south, and saw to her horror that the approaching tarmac had disappeared, and that there was only grass beneath her window. The aircraft was now only about fifty feet above the ground.

There was a large rev of engines, and the Captain put the nose up and off they went back through the clouds, aborting the landing!

The Captain quickly advised that he had aborted the landing, as a huge side wind gust, was pushing the plane over towards the terminal and off the runway.

"It's standard procedure, everyone. Please do not worry. We're going to a calmer area for a while, and wait until the storm leaves the airport area."

The plane circled for over half an hour around the Bay of Islands, not far from another familiar airline also flying from Melbourne that was also circling.

Finally, the Captain advised that the super squall had passed and that clearance had been given to land.

Wendy, for the first time, felt nervous as the plane approached the runway for the second time. The clouds were still low, and it was still bumpy as the terminal appeared in the distance.

A perfect landing! Phew!

Wendy's Kiwi niece was wide eyed as we were greeted by the family.

"Auntie Wendy, we saw the plane come out of the clouds to land, wheels down--and suddenly whoosh, you went up again back into the clouds. I cried, because I thought you had decided not to come after all!"

A passenger in the ticket office, one day, confronted Wendy about the number of hours on each flight for her journey from Melbourne to London Heathrow.

Wendy explained that the first flight was approximately eight hours, followed by a two hour break in transit before the next direct flight to London which would take approximately thirteen hours, the total journey being twenty three hours.

"I can't drink on board then on the flights!" was the response.

"Oh, you don't want to drink alcohol on-board?" replied Wendy.

"No drinks at all, because I can only use a toilet in Transit waiting for the second plane."

Curiosity got the better of Wendy who responded, "So you only want to use the toilets at the airports on your trip? You know there are plenty of toilets on board the aircraft which you can use, except during take-off and landing and if the seat belt sign is on during turbulence."

The lady blushed and replied, "Oh, I thought you had to stay strapped in your seat all the time!"

There was a visible look of relief on her face as she added, "Oh good, so I can have my glass of wine at mealtime!"

Another amusing experience on-board international flights at night time, is the inherent desire for the few to get up suddenly, and rush to a place that they have spotted with three or four empty seats.

Clutching a blanket and pillow, they almost stampede down the aisle to beat others trying to get the same empty row.

They get there to find that one passenger is already seated there, having a midnight snack and drink.

This passenger is quizzed, "Oh, is this your seat?"

"Yes," is the response, and the passenger points to the next seat and adds, "and this seat is my wife's, who is currently waiting in the queue at the toilet!"

The 'seat poachers' then shuffle back down the aisle to their designated seat, sometimes finding another poacher trying to grab the empty seats they had left behind!

One really annoying habit of a minority of passengers takes place when boarding an aircraft.

There are always one or two who block the aisle, deliberately pushing bags into more than one overhead locker. They not only use the one above their seat, but usually the one opposite.

Generally Dave and Wendy have been affected by this practice, when their overhead locker is full, when they open it to put in their carry-on baggage.

"Whose baggage is this?" we ask politely.

"Um, mine, why?" is the answer from the person seated in the seat opposite the aisle. "I didn't have enough room for mine in the locker above me."

It never takes long for the staff on-board to quickly advise the offending passenger that the extra bags need to go under the seat in front of him, or in the cargo hold.

Problem fixed!

Of course, everyone who has flown regularly would have experienced the 'selfish' passenger who pushes back their seat to full extent at meal times when you are trying to eat. There is no room to stand up your glass on the table, let alone get food off the plate in front of you.

There's always friction with screaming children on flights, especially during the night. It is hard for passengers to control their anger at disturbed sleep. Generally, baby's ears can be affected by the change in cabin pressure, which is something that parents can't control.

Obviously by this time, our readers can think of dozens of annoying passengers, especially young children, running around the aisles, not being controlled by their parents.

Needless to say, that in today's large airbus A380s for example, there are around 300 passengers locked inside for hours at a time, all with different personalities, temperaments, demands, idiosyncrasies and habits.

We reckon this adds to the joys of flying!

Body Bits

A coffin inside a wooden crate went missing in Sydney for a week. The bereaved family was naturally upset and angry. The funeral directors were furious. The freight staff involved were also baffled. They remembered seeing the crate when the cargo was checked into their store. They had visions of it been misdelivered and that it might have been sitting in one of the many bond stores on the airport.

Renovations were being done to the bond store at the time. There were quite a few outside workers around. A week later, over in a far corner of the store, some of the renovation workers were eating their lunch seated on a large crate, draped with a tarpaulin. An astute clerk asked them if he could disturb them. He lifted the tarpaulin and discovered that this was the missing coffin.

The workers had been having their coffee breaks on the coffin during the last week. They were all very upset. Strangely enough, not one of them finished their lunch that day!

A friend from another airline told us about this 'body bits' experience.

Janet was working in the city ticket office as a supervisor. One of the staff was making a booking for an elderly man who travelled each year back to Europe to visit his family. This particular trip, he reserved only one seat. The ticket officer politely asked if he needed the usual two seats, one for himself, the other for his wife.

"Not this time love. My wife died six months ago. But I'm still going."

The clerk expressed her sympathies and completed the reservations. She was stunned when the man said, "I won't be lonely though, because my Jean will be with me."

"Of course Mr Brown, your late wife will always be with you in spirit!" was the polite response.

The old man shook his head, put his carry bag up onto the counter and calmly said, "No dear, you don't understand. Jean still goes everywhere with me. She enjoys the outings. I just know she'll enjoy the visit to the old country next month." With those words, he happily pulled out a plastic urn from his bag, which was labelled Jean Brown, cremated 10 June 1986!

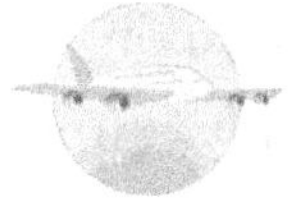

Again, back in the 1970s, Dave's company was handling an aircraft flying to Rome via Tel Aviv every Tuesday.

There was a coffin booked on the flight to Tel Aviv. Because of extra security, a visual check of the remains had to be done at Melbourne airport in the warehouse before the coffin could be put in the cargo hold.

An area at the back of the warehouse was cordoned off and local security in the presence of the airline cargo manager, along with customs and quarantine had to visually and physically inspect the remains for any signs of suspicious objects inside the coffin and on and inside the remains!

This was one of the worst duties of the airline management but a necessary security precaution during the heightened tensions at the time in the Middle East.

When Wendy was handling large commercial business clients at an agency in Melbourne, one of her clients came back from his first class trip with quite a tale to tell. John sipped on his cup of coffee as he told Wendy of his experience.

He was travelling to New York for a conference as a guest speaker. The trip was only for a few days.

Flying from Melbourne to Los Angeles via Auckland, he was seated next to a very large American gentleman who was returning home from a conference in Melbourne.

"Wendy, we got on very well. After eating dinner, we bedded down in our layback seats with blankets over us for some sleep before the flight landed in Los Angeles. Old Charlie was a bit restless next to me, but finally settled down, and I drifted off to sleep."

We should explain that first class flights in the earlier days of the 1980s didn't have the flat beds, but had fairly relaxing large reclining seats.

John continued, "A few hours later, Charlie started to make some peculiar noises. I turned my light on, and nudged him, but he wouldn't wake up. His face was a dreadful colour, so I quickly pulled the call button. The Purser came, took one look, and then rushed off to get a doctor, who was a passenger on board. It was only a minute later when a young man came into first class from the business class section behind us. I got out of my seat, and went and sat in a crew seat."

John took a gulp of his coffee before continuing. "By that time, the doctor was shaking his head. The purser looked shocked, and came over to me and told me that he couldn't offer me any other seat on the aircraft, as the flight was full in all classes."

John then said, the Captain came out and had a quiet chat to the purser and the doctor.

"The captain shook hands with me and said that he was very sorry, but Charlie had died of a massive heart attack. The unfortunate thing was that the DC10 aircraft was beyond the point of being able to divert to Honolulu, and had to continue on for the next two and a half hours to Los Angeles. He was unable to offer me any other seat on the aircraft, so he suggested that I could have a stiff whisky and would have to sit next to the now dead Charlie for the rest of the journey!"

Wendy shook her head.

"John, how did you cope?"

"Well, let's say I had a few whiskies, but I couldn't sleep, so I sat and tried to read a book for the rest of the trip. The airline was terrific. They've offered me a refund for the trip, and they won't take your agency's commission from you. Talk about having a few stiff drinks, whilst travelling next to a stiff!"

Charter Chatter

Dave was transferred to Port Moresby, Papua New Guinea, for one-month back in 1972. He was given a familiarisation ticket up to Mount Hagen in the highlands. To get back to Port Moresby on time for his next shift, the only flights available were from Madang via Lae to Port Moresby. To get to Madang, he had to hitch a lift on an empty DC3 rice charter aircraft. There were no seats, so he stood behind the crew hanging on to anything he could. Wow what a flight that was! Two days later, the local manager came to him at Port Moresby and pulled him to one side. He told Dave that he was responsible for the airline losing a Rice Charter contract to the highlands. The manager explained, "Your extra weight was queried in the figures." The people who had chartered the plane had been given papers which included a charge for Dave's weight--20 bags of rice!

In the mid-eighties, Wendy was working for an international cargo airline which had scheduled services into Sydney and Melbourne, with the 747 aircraft ferrying empty to Hong Kong to join the scheduled cargo services back to Los Angeles, the home port.

Other times, the aircraft would ferry empty to another port for a special charter, where a company or companies chartered the aircraft from that port full of special freight, e.g. computers, or even livestock to another city or country.

One such chartered 747 aircraft was carrying breeding cattle to Taipei from Melbourne, after the scheduled service had been emptied in Melbourne.

Unlike a passenger aircraft, where the 'turnaround' can be as short as an hour, the turnaround was a lot longer. In this case, the crew that flew in the aircraft went to a city hotel for their minimum 12 hour rest.

During this time, the handling agent, plus the charter agent's staff, including a 'load master' were busy working at the airport, directing in and out trucks full of the cattle that had been held in nearby paddocks during the day.

The airline had only two staff in Melbourne; Wendy and the manager. Wendy worked from 9 am to 5 pm but on this day, worked until 7 pm, and then went home after her manager arrived to supervise the charter. The flight was scheduled to depart around 11 pm.

At 8.30 the next morning, Wendy was driving on the road from Sunbury, when she noticed the aircraft on the tarmac at the cargo area!

As soon as she arrived at the office, everyone tried to tell her the tale at the same time.

Finally, she realised there were empty cattle pens on the tarmac, with the cargo agents cleaning them out. The cattle had been returned to their holding yards.

Her manager was still in the office, looking very tired.

"What a night! Everything went smoothly. I was standing outside to record the lift-off time for the departure message. The aircraft was nearly halfway down the runway, when there was a sudden roar to the engines. The plane started to slow down, smoke coming from the wheels as the crew finally pulled up, right at the end of the North-South runway!"

"An aborted take-off. Why?" Wendy asked.

"You know the aircraft 816 had a bit of a nose wobble reported last month. Nothing was found to be wrong when the mechanics checked it. But apparently, under this maximum load, nearing the halfway mark, approaching the rotate speed, the whole front of the cabin shook like mad. The Captain aborted the take-off."

The plane wasn't in its usual position, and had been towed over to the Qantas engineering shed for maintenance and repair.

The engineer who had been on the flight came into the office and finished the tale.

"Wendy, you should have seen the inside of the cabin after we stopped! Our sandwich snacks, which we were going to have after we reached cruising altitude, were splattered around the cabin. The Captain couldn't see the speed of the aircraft when we were stopping, because the shaking had dislodged the instrument panel, hiding the instruments!"

Wendy's manager then added, "When I rushed out to the plane after it had stopped, we were promptly told by the crew not to go near the wheels because they were very hot after the heavy breaking, and the bolts might 'pop' - a deadly weapon! Finally after about ten minutes, we could go up a stairway to the main door. The sight was unbelievable inside the main deck. A few quiet 'moo's' from the cattle--they were remarkably calm, considering the air-conditioning ducts above them had fallen down onto their pens."

Obviously, it took quite a while to tow the plane slowly back to the cargo area, and allow the runway to be cleared for air traffic again. It also took a few hours to unload the pens via the main deck loader, back onto the ground, after the air-conditioning ducts had been lifted back into their correct positions.

The end result was that the aircraft was in maintenance for a few days, getting a new nose wheel. The 'faulty' one was sent back on the next freighter to Los Angeles to be thoroughly checked.

The cattle charter was finally reloaded two days later, on a different aircraft which had been repositioned from Los Angeles to Melbourne, principally for this charter. This time, everything went like clockwork, and the cattle were apparently quite calm again. It was reported that they had settled in very happily in their new country, after their 'mooooving' experience.

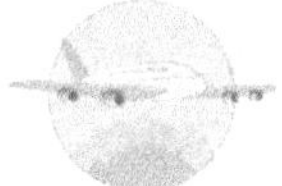

Back in the 80s, Dave's company was chosen to handle a live pig charter to Colombo, Sri Lanka.

An old DC8 freighter from South America landed the day before loading was to commence. The load master was a dubious looking person and the flight engineer was the same.

On the day of the loading, the pigs were loaded into their pens without incident, and then loaded onto the aircraft, starting with the two pens positioned at the front of the aircraft.

The next pens to be loaded were pushed halfway down the aircraft, with the other pens loaded up to the door. Then the first pens on were pushed to the rear of the aircraft.

This procedure was followed to stop the aircraft tail from tipping and hitting the tarmac. Gradually, the rest of the pens were loaded.

As the aircraft was being refuelled, fuel was leaking from the wings. The supervisor of the cargo handling agent's ground staff immediately reported this to the flight engineer, who simply shrugged his shoulders and said, "Everything will be alright!"

The flight engineer then signed off on the fuel. The aircraft eventually took off for Colombo.

Fuel stops had to be made at Darwin, Jakarta, Singapore, Calcutta and Madras, to allow for the fuel leakage in the wings.

Obviously the charterer didn't want to pay top price for an airline like Wendy's, who worked strictly according to safety legislation. If they had used an airworthy 747 freighter, the poor pigs would only have had to refuel at Perth, Western Australia, ending up in a much shorter flight, not stopping in hot places.

Telexes arrived from Colombo the next day, advising that 75 per cent of the pigs had arrived safely. The rest had died en-route!

Just goes to show that cutting costs and corners does not pay.

One of the crew of Wendy's cargo airline related this amazing story of a live cattle charter of breeding cattle from Melbourne to Harbin in the far north east region of China.

The aircraft flew via Shanghai for a fuelling stop for the 747 freighter.

The cattle had been loaded at Melbourne into man-made wooden crates on the tarmac, and then lifted up to the main deck via the main deck loader. The belly hold (the old passenger baggage hold) was loaded by another tarmac loader.

Melbourne airport had all the modern equipment of the day. Harbin airport had nothing for servicing such a large freighter, but obviously the runway and airport of Harbin could handle passenger 747 aircraft.

It was a unique experience for the crew on-board as they taxied towards the unloading area located in the middle of nowhere in the countryside near a small village.

What looked like an 'army of human ants' appeared. A huge man-made wooden structure was slowly pushed on wheels towards the front of the aircraft, when the nose was opened.

The belly loaded cattle were exited via a normal lower deck loader.

The crew grabbed cameras and watched in wonder as the huge team of workers chocked the wooden ramp's wheels, and then walked up the ramp to meet their fellow workers who were now inside the main deck.

The first pens in the nose were carefully opened, and one by one, each animal was tethered and escorted down the long wide ramp by two or three men, who led them onto the tarmac then across the grass and up short ramps onto waiting trucks. Other workers inside the aircraft dismantled the rest of the crates, and carried the planks down the long ramp then stacked them in a pile on the grass. The next set of crates were then moved forward to the now empty front row, ready to be dismantled and the next animals tethered to be led down the ramp, and so on. Some of the cattle were actually handed over to their new owner or owners, who had presented their paperwork to the Chinese customs official, and walked their new breeding animal across the fields towards their village.

The experience was like being in a 'time-warp' with the worker ants, moving each animal off the aircraft expertly. The engineer who related this tale still couldn't believe how accurately the man-made ramp had been made to lock onto the aircraft nose without a millimetre out of place. It was all done by measurements provided by the airline.

The crew finally left the tarmac for their twelve hour crew rest, before flying the aircraft the next day empty to Hong Kong to reposition it for a scheduled service to Los Angeles.

To their amazement, every single piece of the ramp and the crates had disappeared when they arrived back at the aircraft the next morning. The army of workers had also disappeared back to their homes. The aircraft was parked where they had left it, with only the re-fuellers standing by.

Normally, in Australia, the airports provided a jumbo 'super sucker' which was like an enormous vacuum cleaner attached to a tanker, which cleaned out the debris left behind in the cargo holds.

The army of workers had spent the night hand cleaning the interior. Mick, the engineer, reckoned that they did a better job than the jumbo sucker.

Apparently, all the wood went to the workers homes and families for their own use, for building, burning, etc. as the countryside was basically open plains, with very few trees for wood.

Such is life in the remote areas of the world.

Late one evening, Wendy was working on the tarmac, assisting her manager with a horse charter destined for Singapore.

There were the usual 'horsey' hangers-on standing on the tarmac, starting to get in the way of the loading.

Wendy had the weather and flight plans in her hand which she had just collected from the main terminal.

She went to go up the steps, which led to the main deck. Her path was blocked by two of the 'horsey' people, namely two young women who were sitting on the steps, drinking coffee from thermos flasks.

"Excuse me, but could you please move off these steps and finish your coffee away from the aircraft and tarmac," asked Wendy.

Wendy received two blank defiant stares. "Why, we booked this aircraft!"

"Correction, your father, who's the charter agent, chartered the flight for the racing owners, who are all inside where they belong. This area is actually out of bounds for security reasons."

"Why should we move? Who are you anyway!" responded the ginger headed lass, not moving an inch.

Wendy politely responded, "Well, you don't have security passes on you, and I have an ID security pass for the tarmac and this happens to be the airline that I work for, and the Captain and crew are waiting for me to come up these stairs and go to the cockpit to receive their paperwork that I've got for them." Wendy pointed towards the Captain who was now standing at the top of the stairs at the main door.

"Ah, so Wendy's finally getting you two to move?" he said. "We need the steps to be used for staff only!"

Without another word, the two girls got up, clattered down the steps and were escorted by one of the tarmac workers over to the main cargo terminal door and ushered through the terminal to the car park out the front.

Such people can be the bane of the airlines, especially when handling a chartered aircraft. These girls were in danger of being injured on the tarmac, by equipment movement and also a possible skittish horse!

Crew Capers

Working for a cargo airline has many funny moments. The crews assigned to these 747 Jumbo aircraft were senior officers at the top of the company bid line. Naturally, they chose to travel out from their home base in America to the land of Oz as frequently as possible.

Part of Wendy's job was to organise the hotel and crew rest for the Captain, First Officer, Maintenance Engineer and Charter Supervisor. They normally had an overnight stay before flying the aircraft back to an Asian port, either empty, to reposition for a scheduled flight, or full as a chartered flight.

One Senior 'check' Captain was often in Melbourne. Captain Jim always arrived looking more like a tourist than a Captain. When Wendy or her station manager met the aircraft and climbed the stairs up to the cabin, there was Jim casually seated, finishing a cup of coffee, wearing shorts and t-shirt! Apparently that's the way this Captain preferred to travel. "I just hate uniforms and collar and ties!" Much to Wendy's amusement, Jim disappeared into the toilet and re-appeared some minutes later, in full uniform ready to face the 'public domain'. Guess the clothes don't make a good pilot!

Strangely enough, another Captain used to fly late at night in his striped pyjamas!

Travelling back from a Cargo Course in Los Angeles, Wendy and her counterpart officer from Sydney were sitting upstairs in the Freighter, Boeing 747. No frills in the cargo aircraft--the stairs were a retractable ladder leading up from the main deck. The main deck on passenger 747's were beautifully lined, with lush ceilings, walls and overhead lockers, and toilets etcetera to make it comfortable for passengers to travel. The freighter, 'downstairs' on the main deck was not lined--you could see all the mechanics in the aircraft.

Wendy and Jenny made themselves comfortable upstairs. This section looked just like a normal 'old fashioned' first class section--which in fact it was, as a converted passenger aircraft bought from another airline. They had comfortable seats, (12 seats in all) plus they had a toilet, galley (which was self-service) complete with microwave ovens.

Not long before take-off, the Captain, First Officer, Flight Engineer, and the Maintenance Engineer boarded. Jenny and Wendy knew the crew, because they organised their accommodation for overnight stays in Sydney and Melbourne, plus their jobs included getting the weather and flight information from the control people at their respective Airport, and give them to the Captain for each flight from Australia. The crew had become friends over the years.

The Maintenance Engineer, a fun guy who came from San Francisco, grinned and said, "I've got a special drink for you two for your trip home." He produced a coat hanger, with a plastic bag taken from an Australian Wine Flask!

It was hung in the locker at the back of the passenger cabin, for them to 'tipple' from as desired.

Obviously, the crew were tea-total, as per regulations throughout the flight which went via Honolulu, Fiji and Sydney to Melbourne.

Wendy had one little last sip from the still nearly full cask bladder an hour out of Melbourne. It was a nice gesture from a lovely man who knew that they didn't have alcohol served, like it was on a normal passenger flight.

During the night on the same flight where Wendy and Jenny had their special 'wine on tap', the Captain came out of the flight deck and saw that Wendy was awake.

"Hey Wendy, want to see something really special in the sky in ten minutes?"

The answer was of course in the affirmative.

Wendy and the Captain tried to stir the heavily sleeping Jenny, but only received a grumpy, "Go away, lemme sleep!"

Wendy went into the flight deck and sat behind the Captain.

Ten minutes later, an amazing sight appeared in the black clear night sky ahead in the far distance. It was *Halley's Comet,* which is not seen from earth very often.

Everyone in the flight deck sat, literally stunned by the beauty of the comet as it trekked across the southern hemisphere's skies, leaving a crystal clear trail behind it.

A familiar passenger aircraft was flying at a different altitude ahead of their aircraft. An Australian accent came over the earphones on Wendy's headset. It was the Captain of the Qantas airline. "Hey folks. What a sight eh? One chance in a million and we Aussies and you Americans were privileged to see it. Enjoy the rest of your flight."

The Captain on Wendy's flight, laughed and responded, "Sure was, mate! A perfect view for us. Hope some of your passengers were awake to see it too? By the way, there's one of our Aussie staff, sitting behind me that saw it too!"

Nice to hear such friendship in the skies!

Wendy remained in the flight deck as it wasn't long before dawn, and that was the time the aircraft, which was fully laden with freight, had to land and refuel at Nadi, Fiji. The scheduled freighter service normally flew from Los Angeles, via Honolulu, then direct to Sydney then to Melbourne, Wendy's home port.

Once the aircraft entered Fijian airspace, the Nadi control tower personnel contacted the freighter 747 and asked, "Would you like to make a visual landing, East to West?"

"Roger, we'll make a visual landing and approach, if the weather is clear."

"There is some cloud around, but just let us know when you see the beacon along the east coast, as that's where you turn direct West to approach Nadi airport."

"Affirmative - will do!"

The Captain turned the aircraft to the north, following the East Coastline below. Everyone peered out of the windshield, looking for the beacon. During this time, the Captain handed over the controls to his co-pilot, who had landed the previous week at Nadi, and was therefore more familiar with the local territory.

The co-pilot weaved the big 747 around the large fluffy cumulus clouds ahead so they could see the coast clearly. Eventually, there was a chorus, "There it is!"

The aircraft was then turned towards the east, and now faced the rising sun.

"Tigers 419 to control--turning west at the beacon and now on flight path to Nadi airport. Will advise when we see the airport for visual landing."

"Nadi Control to Tigers. The current temperature is 95 degrees Fahrenheit and nil wind, with visual approach."

The Captain nodded at the co-pilot and said, "Take it easy Jo, we're very heavy, and this heat and humidity could make it a heavy landing!"

"Okay, Captain!"

Fifteen minutes later, the aircraft lumbered down through the sky on its approach. The Captain called out the height from the tarmac once they were over the perimeter fence. "One hundred--eighty--fifty--thirty--fifteen--ten--five..."

Thump--bang--bounce. Finally the aircraft settled onto the deck, the reverse thrusts roared and the brakes were applied.

The Captain looked over at Jo, the co-pilot, who grinned at him and said, "Oops, sorry, Hank. Hell that was a heavy landing!"

Captain Hank grinned back and replied, "Well, there are no wheels inside the cabin, so we are OK. In the circumstances, a great landing!"

Jenny, who greeted Wendy when she returned to her seat, said, "What on earth has been going on? We seemed to be weaving in and out of the clouds for twenty minutes, then, heck, what a heavy landing!"

They both laughed, after Wendy told her the story.

"Such a pity you didn't want to interrupt your beauty sleep, Jenny, missing the comet!"

Another time, when Wendy was returning to Melbourne on the freighter service from Los Angeles, she was invited up into the flight deck for landing, as the crew knew that she loved to see the landings.

Melbourne is a safe area for a large airport, mainly because of the large, clear flat surroundings, unlike Sydney, where take-offs and landings are more difficult, next to the harbour and being adjacent to the city buildings.

This particular time, the control tower asked the Captain if he wished to practice an automated landing.

"Roger, will do. A good day to do it, as it's rather hazy this morning," was the response.

The Captain and co-pilot prepared the aircraft for the 'automated' landing. To explain--this is when the aircraft involved has the correct electronic equipment to connect direct with the control tower's computer, which then controls the height, speed etc. of the aircraft and the direction onto the tarmac. The crew then take over. Mind you, the crew can opt to take over at any time, if they feel that something is not going to plan.

As the flight approached Melbourne airport, the haze made it very difficult to see clearly in the distance. Everyone peered out through the windshield, searching for the familiar buildings, such as the water tower, control tower and the local motels.

The Captain and co-pilot kept sweeping their eyes over the controls as the aircraft started to descend.

"Sheez, can't see the airport yet!" remarked the co-pilot.

"It's there--we just can't see it yet," replied the Captain, who turned to Wendy and added, "Cross your fingers, girl!" He folded his hands on his lap, and added, "Look, no hands!"

Suddenly, there it was, and by this time, the aircraft was only about one hundred and fifty feet above the fence perimeter.

Wendy gasped as the plane lowered itself gently onto the tarmac with barely a thump! Straight away, the crew took over the controls and applied the reverse thrust and brakes, then taxied it to the cargo terminal.

"This is why we like to practice such landings in relatively good weather, Wendy, because one time we might need to utilise it during a dense fog or a storm." The Captain grinned. "Fun, huh!"

The wonders of modern technology!

Back in the late seventies, a European airline Boeing 707 took off from Melbourne for Sydney thence to Singapore, the Middle East and finally Europe.

The international language used worldwide for crew and control towers is English, when communication is used.

The Captain was asked by the control tower to turn to the north for Sydney after take-off on the East/West runway. This required basically a left turn after take-off.

No-one knew what happened, but the control tower saw the aircraft on its radar turn right and head south for Antarctica!

They quickly ordered the Captain to make a 180 degree turn and head for Sydney.

Thank goodness again for modern technology!

On another occasion in the 80s, a European carrier, flying a Lockheed DC10, lined up to land at Essendon Airport, the secondary airport at Melbourne, which can only cater for lighter and smaller aircraft.

This happened as the control tower kept contacting the crew to confirm if they could see the runway, because they could not see the aircraft visually, and because the radar was indicating that they were 'off-course'.

"We can see the runway ahead. There appears to be a tram track running along the perimeter!" was the response from the crew.

"Abort your landing--you are lining up on Essendon Airport! Climb immediately to a thousand feet and make a left turn, then we'll direct you back to Melbourne Tullamarine."

Phew, nearly a bad landing! The DC10 would have cracked the runway because of its size and weight. The plane could have potentially stranded there--or worse still, not been able to pull up in time and crashed into housing.

A similar incident happened a couple of years earlier, when an Asian carrier actually landed a DC8 onto the tarmac at Essendon. Fortunately, the airport had the tarmac facilities for such an aircraft. Unfortunately, the passengers had to stay on board until buses came with customs and immigration officials to process them, after they climbed down the single stairway to the terminal.

The crew stayed on board, ready to fly the empty aircraft back to Tullamarine, six kilometres away!

During this time, the baggage, cargo and mail was offloaded, and trucked to Tullamarine.

The passengers were eventually sent by coach to Tullamarine for final clearances into the country.

One dark and moonless night, an Asian carrier was heading toward Melbourne from Sydney.

The control tower was tracking the flight on the radar as it approached Mount Macedon thirty odd kilometres to the north of Tullamarine airport.

Normally, aircraft travelled over the Mount at a higher altitude. This time, the control tower noticed that the crew were descending too early, and were heading straight for the mountain top.

The control tower immediately ordered the crew to ascend to a higher altitude to avoid the mountain top.

Just after this order was carried out, the crew saw a large illuminated cross ahead, which, as they ascended, disappeared below them as they passed over it.

Folk lore tales from the locals on the mount, claim they could hear the roar of the engines as it passed over that night. They obviously only cleared the Mount Macedon Memorial Cross by a few hundred feet. This meant that the plane would have hit the mountain if they had not been diverted by the astute control tower staff on duty!

The air traffic controllers have an unenviable job. They are the unsung heroes of airlines and their work is not often acknowledged.

Recently, when Wendy and Dave were visiting family in Scotland, they flew in over Scandinavia en-route to Glasgow.

The Captain announced, "Good morning everyone. If you have a look on your screens through the belly camera, we are currently flying over Denmark. Thought you might like to see the snow that you are flying into! It's apparently going to be heavy snow, and very cold when we land at Glasgow."

Wow! He wasn't wrong. One could say it was a winter wonderland below.

When they finally reached the approach to land at Glasgow, Wendy and Dave looked at the nose camera, and could only see white. It was literally a 'white-out'.

The Captain brought in the aircraft via automated landing. He didn't use any brakes, just reverse thrust to slow down. It was a perfect landing, but a spooky sight looking out the window at the blizzard outside!

Coming back to Australia after enjoying the cold and snow of Scotland and Europe, Wendy and Dave were on the final fourteen hour leg from Dubai to Melbourne.

They were both suffering from colds. Dave slept like a log, much to Wendy's disgust, as she could not sleep or lie down flat on the bed, because it affected her asthma which was bad because of her cold.

Suddenly, Wendy developed night cramps in her calves. She hobbled back to the bar area and asked for tonic water.

The crew were terrific. She was supplied with snacks and plenty of small cans of tonic water.

The stewardess said, "This has happened to you before, I see," pointing to Wendy's bare feet on the bar floor. "I was just going to suggest walking on the cool floor in bare feet!"

Wendy kept the crew occupied for the next few hours as she restlessly walked up and down the aircraft to relieve the cramps. Eventually, after the wonderful help of the crew, the cramps had gone--but so had most of Wendy's sleep!

Custom Cuties

Obviously, there are many cute stories emanating from the Custom areas at international airports. People will try to bring all sorts of banned or illegal items into Australia. Most plead ignorance of the local laws; others bring in items on good faith.

One good faith incident occurred in the passenger terminal. The customs officer was checking in a European flight full of immigrants and visiting relatives. Customs were doing their routine spot checks of luggage and their contents.

One elderly couple had several large suitcases. An interpreter on duty advised them that the officer wanted them to open the suitcases. They happily obliged. The first three cases were full of clothes and personal belongings. The last small bag was then opened. Inside there were at least two dozen bottles. The officer picked up one of the bottles. The bottle dropped accidentally from his grasp and smashed into pieces on the floor. Chaos erupted around the bench as the custom officer and his co-workers ran around stomping on the live leaches, whilst the elderly couple tried to stop them and recollect them! Quarantine eventually collected all the offending leeches and confiscated them.

The translator hurriedly translated for the old couple. "We brought the leeches in for our son to use to 'bleed' his sick mother in law! It's normal custom back in our country!"

After one of their trips to the UK to visit family, Wendy and Dave were fully prepared for the Quarantine inspection upon arrival in Melbourne.

Whilst in the UK, they had visited a famous deer park. This was during a 'foot and mouth' scare throughout the country.

Even though they had followed all the precautions of walking through disinfectant sponges at the gates on entry and exit, they were aware that Quarantine in Melbourne would still want to inspect and disinfect the shoes worn on that day, plus any other shoes worn on farm visits.

They had deliberately put these shoes into plastic bags in the top of their suit cases. They had also ticked the part on the entry forms stating that they had visited a farm where the deer park was situated in Leicester. The deer on that farm were actually being bred for the Royal Family.

The Quarantine man sighed with relief when he saw how prepared they were.

"Thanks, guys. It's been frantic here this morning, as a lot of people have come in from the UK and have been on farms and such. We've had to spend extra time going through all their luggage, check for possible contaminated shoes and clothing. You've made my job easy!" he said with a big grin. "I won't be a minute. I've just got to spray these shoes, and then you can go."

While Wendy and Dave waited, they watched in amusement at other passengers fumbling in suitcases and carry-on baggage, trying to find their shoes that were needed by Quarantine.

There were clothes all over the floor, and people bumping into each other. Some were getting very irritable at the delay.

But, as they had been politely advised by the airport personnel, the disinfection was to stop the 'foot and mouth' disease coming into Australia.

They recognised some fellow passengers from their flight, who were still searching for certain shoes. These passengers waved at them, one saying, "Heck, we wish we were prepared like you two!"

Guess the advantage of airline 'inside knowledge' was our saviour that day.

Such inside knowledge helped the Laings on most entries back into Melbourne from overseas.

They were always very careful when completing the Immigration Entry Forms, making sure they declared the exact amounts of overseas purchases, ready for inspection if required. They also had all the receipts ready to show.

Too many times, they witnessed people arguing with the Customs Officers, pretending that they 'Didn't know' or 'Oh I don't understand' or they even tried to get sympathy or try to talk their way around the Australian regulations.

When working for the American International Air Cargo Airline, Wendy dealt with Customs and Quarantine Officers every time her airline arrived or departed. The plane was parked at the cargo area of Tullamarine Airport, away from the passenger terminal.

These staff drove down to the aircraft and went on board with Wendy to 'clear' the Captain, Co-pilot, Engineer and Maintenance Engineer into Melbourne. The crew always took a minimum twenty-four hour rest at a city hotel, before flying out another aircraft the next day.

That day, of course, another crew who had been staying in Melbourne arrived by taxi to the cargo terminal, and were then cleared by the same Customs, Quarantine, and Immigration officials for the aircraft departure.

Thus Wendy and Dave, who was the Airline's Cargo Handling Agent's supervisor, were well aware of the duties of these officers.

Some of these officers obviously became 'Tarmac Friends'.

Speaking about 'Tarmac Friends'--sometimes 'inside jokes' were played on the authors.

This all occurred back in the 80s, before the current strict security regulations were imposed.

On one occasion, an antique oak bureau that Wendy had inherited from her first late husband's family in the UK was sent as Airline employee discount cargo from Manchester to Melbourne.

Wendy had utilised a Cargo Agent to pack, clear customs and send the bureau. The same agent's Melbourne office cleared the bureau through Customs in Melbourne, and sent it on to a furniture restorer in Melbourne.

The bureau was in good nick, but needed some hinges repaired.

Wendy was notified by the airline that the bureau had arrived, and was en-route to the furniture restorer.

The next morning, she received a phone call from the furniture man.

"Wendy, there's something odd about your bureau."

"Oh, what's wrong?"

"Well, it's beautifully packed and sealed. When we opened it, there was newspaper packing inside, which was understandable, because that would protect the lead light glass on the side doors. However, when they opened the doors, there were some empty Fosters' Beer cans inside--nicely wrapped too--plus a note. I'll read it to you. It says, 'The Phantom has struck' and that's all it said! Does this mean anything to you?"

Wendy laughed, "Oh yes, that note and the cans are obviously Customs friends playing a joke on me. They have the ability of opening and closing containers, packages and parcels without showing that that has been done, especially if the Federal Police need to look inside for drugs to trace the drug consignee. Wait 'till I see them tomorrow!"

Similar jokes were played on other airline staff by the baggage handlers.

On one occasion, friends placed some wrapped bricks in a suitcase belonging to an airline employee who was going on his honeymoon with his new wife.

When he arrived at his destination, he struggled with the weight of the case, and then, Customs asked for the suitcase to be opened during a spot check.

One can only imagine the astonishment on the officers' faces and also the airline employee, when the bricks were discovered.

Not much needed to be explained in those days, and everyone had a good laugh!

Food Fun

Good friends of ours who were also in the airline industry departed on their honeymoon to a Pacific Island. Unknown to them, their co-workers had ordered 'special' meals for them.

After being presented with a nice bottle of Champagne, an announcement was made over the intercom for all passengers to hear. "Congratulations to the newlyweds, Jack & Jill. We have a special treat that we wish to give them for their dessert!"

Down came their 'special meals' covered by lids. Naturally, surrounding passengers were keen to see what was so special. There were shrieks and hoots of approving laughter all round as Jack and Jill pulled off the lids covering their dishes to expose carefully arranged collations of fruit cheese and jelly! Jack's was a cleverly designed woman's body, complete with two wobbly pink jelly 'boobs' with cherries atop each mound. Jill's 'man' came complete with a large peeled erect banana looming up from between large peach halves!

Dave and Wendy were married three months later and were naturally VERY wary when they received their first meal on board. They were on their honeymoon trip on board the 'opposition', and as jokes were often played on such occasions--for example, dinner has been known to be served to airline staff honeymooners; cabbage with a large sausage to the man and two rounded spoons of pink jelly with a cherry atop each one to the lady, amid giggles from the crew and other passengers. So no wonder they were a little nervous as the purser approached with a tray, covered over with a napkin, obviously hiding something tall beneath it!

Wrong! They were presented a lovely bottle of expensive French bubbly! A gesture appreciated and often reciprocated around the industry. Despite the fact that International airlines compete with each other at the business end there was a nice rapport between the airlines at Melbourne airport during their working days at the terminal. Everyone shared each other's joys and each other's sorrows. Catering departments were always willing accomplices when a fellow airline worker was to be feted on a special occasion.

Wendy worked during her last years with International airlines in the city office.

One shift involved working on the pre-flight check list for passengers. One of the main requirements was to check passengers who didn't have contact details in Australia or no incoming or outgoing flight details. Such lack of information meant that the passenger had booked through other airlines, or direct, with several airlines on different days. They were basically 'hogging' seats on several flights, then making up their minds at the last minute.

This meant that all airlines, for example at Christmas, high season, cancelled these passengers off the flight, to 'shake down' the overbooked flight list.

One of the other interesting jobs on this roster during the week involved sending off messages to the home port, requesting special meals for passengers, known in the industry as SPML requests.

Meals like diabetic diets, low calorie, low fat, low potassium, religious diets and the like where all attended to on this roster.

One passenger's mother, who had visited the ticket office and talked to Wendy the previous day, had specifically asked for a special meal request, which wasn't catered for in the normal special meal requests.

Her six year old son was travelling from Melbourne the next weekend to London via Hong Kong with her, and he only would drink milk and eat Vegemite sandwiches!

This meant that Wendy had to advise the caterers at Melbourne Airport, Hong Kong Airport and London Airport, to provide this meal request for her son. London Airport was involved, as they were returning from London via Hong Kong back to Melbourne, three weeks later. Their full return trip would reflect the meal requests in their bookings and would alert each station to prepare the meals to take on board for each flight.

Vegemite is basically an Australian product. Hong Kong, at that time, had to 'pre-position' a jar of vegemite for this boy on an earlier flight from Australia. The same applied to the London caterers.

One can only say that Wendy held her breath, when four weeks later, the mother came into the ticket office and asked to see Wendy.

Phew! She gave Wendy a box of chocolates as a thank you present. We wonder if this boy, now a man, possibly with children of his own, has the same problem!

One time, when Wendy and Dave were flying to the UK to see his family, he was on a medical low potassium diet.

This diet was very restrictive; and as such, root foods like potato, carrots, pumpkin etc. had to be double boiled and the liquid discarded. Tomatoes, bananas, avocados, and kiwi fruits, were banned also, which made a very bland diet!

The airline did well and produced the correct food, which was very plain. At home, during the two years Dave was on this diet, garlic or onion powder was added to the potatoes etc. to add flavour.

Dave started drooling at Wendy's meals on board whilst he ate boiled chicken and salad.

On the return flight, Dave dreaded the thought of bland food all the way home again, so he cheated a little bit.

We know that his kidney specialist knew this would happen, but praised Dave for his diligence.

Fortunately upon return to Melbourne, the date was finally set for his kidney transplant from Wendy.

A couple of years later, they travelled back to the UK and Europe, and Dave ate heartily on board!

Dave was a passenger on a European airline, flying to Singapore via Karachi.

When the dinner was served en route to Karachi, a lot of the passengers, including Dave, were served pork, which was the only choice on board.

The two men sitting either side of Dave refused the meal, as did other passengers, who were obviously destined for Karachi, and their religious dietary requirements had not been considered by the caterers of the airline!

This was a serious 'faux pas' on that airline's behalf!

A similar 'faux pas' occurred when Wendy was travelling from Melbourne to Auckland.

She was travelling on a staff pass in First Class, with her first late husband on his airline.

Lunch was served with appropriate aplomb. The passengers murmured to each other, as they started their meals. Some refused to eat their meal. It was steak and vegetables. There was no other choice on the menu for that short flight.

The caterers and airline had forgotten that the flight was on Good Friday!

Sometime accents can cause problems. Wendy and Dave were flying to Auckland. The steward came round to take their meal orders.

Dave placed his order. Wendy was asked by the steward, "Would you like 'Fush or Chucken?"

"You mean Fish or Chicken?" grinned Wendy.

"Yes, that's what I said - Fush or Chucken!"

The steward suddenly laughed, when he realised that Wendy was taking the mickey out of him!

He continued down the aircraft, being very careful to say, "Fish or Chicken" with a pommy accent.

Some airlines have very limited alcohol beverages on board, and some do not have alcohol at all.

One flight Dave was flying to Singapore via Sydney from Melbourne in first class with an East European airline.

All he was offered was slibovic (plum brandy) or their national wine or beer.

So all Dave drank was orange juice.

Air sick bags are not always found in passengers' seat pockets. Perhaps this is result of limited turnaround times, or perhaps because previous passengers have souvenired them!

Wendy was on one such flight. A passenger in the row in front of her had pressed the call button. A steward came to her.

"I'm feeling very sick! I need a sick bag!"

"I won't be a moment!"

The steward rushed off to the galley, and came back to the passenger. Unfortunately, he was too late! The passenger had been sick.

It took quite a while to clean up not only the passenger, but the seat she was seated on.

Another strange, but true tale on board.

A friend of Wendy and Dave's has told this tale.

She was flying home to Australia from Europe. After boarding, the flight was delayed for nearly an hour at the departure gate, due to a sudden violent storm.

Finally, the aircraft was cleared to leave. The flight was rather bumpy, but the crew diligently started to serve the dinner.

When coffee was served, the plane suddenly went through some more turbulence. Whoops! Coffee went all over her top and lap.

The crew helped her clean up, but she spent the rest of the flight back to Australia, which was twenty-four hours, including a short stop over, reeking of second-hand coffee!

It almost seems to be guaranteed that a flight will hit turbulence when one is trying to eat or drink on board.

Freight Follies

Harry Smith, an old cargo supervisor, used to be a cattle drover and railwayman in Queensland in the early thirties. He had trouble getting his tongue around lots of words. Here are a few examples of his inherent malapropisms:

"We will have to sympathise (synchronise) our watches."

"That young lad Bill is cheeky. He will have to change his altitude (attitude)."

"This cargo must get on the next plane to DESPESPAR (Denpasar)."

"The capital of Indonesia is JAKARATA (Jakarta)."

"That country in central America called Gootemalia (Guatemala)."

"Freight forwarding company called Coogle and Naggel (Kuhne and Nagel)."

"Freight forward company called Panalpalina (Panalpina)."

Aaron, one of the cargo clerks, was famous for his brusque manner, short fuse and short sightedness. He hated doing the front counter shift. His spectacles were thicker than the bottom of a coke bottle! One day a woman came to the front counter carrying a small baby. She said, "I have something to send to Sydney."

Aaron looked at her and replied, "You'll need a pet pack for *that*, Madam," pointing to the baby bundled up in her arms. The woman immediately burst into tears. Aaron had no patience for this sort of behaviour and started to shout at her saying, "There's no choice, Madam. That cat has to go in a pet pack in the cargo hold. You simply cannot take it on board with you."

Fortunately, Frank, the supervisor passing by, realised Aaron's mistake and calmed the woman down. By this time, the baby was crying. Funnily enough, the baby sounded just like a meowing cat!

Richard was an administration supervisor at a Melbourne Airport Cargo Terminal. He was not a very popular man and was always too keen to embarrass or belittle his subordinates. His co-workers decided that enough was enough and that it was time to teach him a lesson in humility.

Richard used a bicycle to peddle to and from the airport. One evening, he went to the spot where he had left his bike. It was gone. Had someone stolen it? His co-workers knew otherwise.

The next morning, more 'all ports' telexes were received than usual. Richard sat down to read them and soon realised what had happened. He had a telex from Darwin in the Northern Territory, "We have a bicycle wheel here with no marks or numbers on it." Another telex came from

Cairns, Queensland that said, "We have a set of bicycle handle bars without marks or numbers." Yet another telex from Perth, Western Australia stated, "We have a pair of bike pedals here with no marks or numbers." And so on...

The chastened Richard sent out an 'all ports' telex in reply: "All those with spare bicycle parts at their station, please return them to Melbourne airport, attention Richard Black."

Three days later with all parts returned; he rode his bicycle home.

Many years ago, Dave was working in the Melbourne city cargo office. He was on shift at 9.00 pm one night. The truck came in from the airport, full of cargo. The first thing to be unloaded was a Petpak with a cat in it. One of the clerks, a cat lover, felt compelled to open the Petpak to look at the pedigree champion inside.

One glance at the stranger's face terrified the already frightened cat. It jumped out of the Petpak and bolted out the open door. It was gone! What were they going to do? The new owner was due there soon to pick up the cat. Dave and his duty supervisor, Frank, decided to go and look for the missing cat. They each grabbed a small parcel sack and headed off up the street with a slim chance of sighting the cat.

Half an hour later, they were in a back alley behind the adjacent brewery, when they spotted a cat which looked like the missing one. It was feeding amongst the rubbish. Frank looked at Dave and smiled. They were running out of time. The owner would be there soon to pick up her new cat.

Frank took a wide berth and gently crept around the other side without disturbing the eating animal. Together they managed to get close enough to toss the bag over the cat and secure it in the bag.

Dave and Frank with big smiles on their faces triumphantly walked back to the office with the cat. The cat was put into the Petpak and the door closed securely. An hour later, the woman walked into the office to enquire after her new breeding cat. She was given the Petpak. She signed for it and left.

They never heard again from that woman. But Dave and Frank knew that she had got an alley cat and not the pedigree one that she was expecting. Obviously, the new sire produced some great progenies.

Not long after the 'bolting cat' episode, an elderly woman brought in a cockatoo in a travel cage to send to her sister in Perth. She knew that the booked flight was not for a few hours. But she would have to leave it at the city office because she had other appointments.

The woman explained that the cockatoo was quite a talker. The cockatoo was placed in the holding area to wait for the truck to take it to the airport with other cargo. Each time Jo, one of the clerks, walked past the bird, he said, "F... off Cocky!" The other staff decided to do the same.

By the time the cockatoo in its cage was loaded onto the truck to go to the airport, it was saying this new phrase repeatedly, looking very pleased with himself. "F... off cocky!"

Goodness knows what the woman's sister thought when she picked up her new pet from Perth airport. Hopefully she had a sense of humour!

Most aircraft, passenger or cargo, often carry some sort of valuable cargo or documents in their hold. Unknown to the passengers, there may be gold bullion for transport interstate or overseas on board their aircraft.

One famous vanishing trick occurred at Melbourne International Airport a few years ago. A brick of gold bullion went missing, despite the fact that the usual armed guard had been employed to supervise the cargo in transit from their company truck, to the cargo shed and thence to the locked container which was put on the aircraft. Each bullion brick was carefully boxed in individual wooden crates and to an unskilled observer's eye, looked like a small shoebox.

Panic buttons were pressed when the precious cargo was unloaded the other end. One piece was missing! Airport security, Federal Police, airline management and staff ran around, but to no avail. Apparently, someone had 'scored' a nice nest egg!

Several months later, one cold winter's day in Melbourne, one of the airline staff in the cargo office felt an annoying draft blowing into the clerk's area. Jo got up, to locate where the draft was coming from. A back door into the cargo shed was propped open. He went to kick the brick aside and nearly broke his toe! The box was opened revealing the missing gold nugget. A cleaner, months prior, had innocently propped the door open using the disguised nugget that had fallen off the trailer onto the floor. Case closed!

Traffic Traumas

The skies can get crowded at times, especially over such airports as New York and Chicago. Even Sydney gets hectic, especially in the morning when international aircraft are getting low on fuel and are requesting landing clearances after a long flight.

Wendy was on board the freighter, coming back from a course in Los Angeles. The crew invited her to sit in the cockpit for landing. Seated in the 'jump seat' immediately behind the Captain on the left side, Wendy listened in with fascination through her headset to the conversation between the air traffic control and the various aircraft due to land at Sydney. The following quotes are not accurate but will give you an idea of what happened.

"Sydney control to Freighters (he, he, nearly gave out airline code name!) You can now descend to three thousand feet and land as soon as possible!"

"Freighter to Sydney control! Are you mad? We are heavy, fully laden with 100 tons of freight. We need more time to descend to landing level! Over!"

A different voice came over the intercom. "Freighter, this is Sydney Control supervisor. Please maintain your present altitude of five thousand feet and hold. We will let Qantas 005 light (i.e. a passenger aircraft) land before you."

They then heard the supervisor calmly advising the controller that a 747 freighter was always much heavier than a passenger 747 and as a result could not descend as fast, because the wings might rip off! The supervisor then 'took over' and gave the appropriate instructions and clearances for descent. They landed without incident after the Qantas flight.

Ironically, the Qantas Captain spoke to the freighter's Captain after the incident, aircraft to aircraft, when they were both on the ground. They couldn't help but laugh at his comment to the freighter's Captain. "Struth mate! I thought for a moment that I was about to witness a 'Freighter' dive bomb!" Again, no airline staff would dream of being an air traffic controller, and have great respect for these people.

Whilst in Hong Kong, on a trip for a staff course, Wendy and her co-worker from Sydney, Mary, were invited to see the company flight simulators. (Airline staff laughingly referred to these huge machines as Flight stimulators!).

They climbed up the steps that led them into the large simulator. Inside they found themselves inside a perfect mock-up of a 747 flight deck.

The company Check Captain, who had given them the invitation, sat in the Captain's seat on the left. Mary sat in the co-pilot's seat and Wendy sat in the jump seat behind the Captain.

"Okay, ladies, let's do a take-off in a cross wind." He then added into his microphone to the controller outside, "Practicing a cross wind take-off."

A voice came through their headsets.

"Cleared for take-off on north south runway two--wind gusting at 70 knots from the north-east."

"Roger," replied the Captain.

It was just like being in a normal aircraft, complete with the small motions of the wheels gathering speed over the imaginary tarmac. There was a sudden movement as the cabin (and imaginary aircraft) was pushed hard to the left (West)--just as if a big gust of wind was blowing the aircraft across the tarmac as it gathered speed.

The Captain steadied the aircraft and then it 'lifted' off the ground. The simulator rose up into the air, just like a real plane.

Wendy and Mary found it hard to believe that they were simply sitting in a big mock-up of a cockpit inside a large hanger! It was so real.

Ten minutes later, they went through the experience of what it would actually feel like to land in a snow storm. Even the view out of the windshield was an exact 'film' of such a landing in Anchorage!

Fortunately, the Check Captain was kind enough not to put them through an experience of very severe turbulence, or the experience of loss of engine power on take-off.

These machines are obviously a great way for pilots to practice such events without actually hurting themselves or passengers. The controller of the simulator often threw 'surprise' events at pilots when they were having their yearly check.

Flight simulators are an essential part of training pilots to expect the unexpected.

Tarmac Tales

The most interesting part of Wendy and Dave's airline careers were spent during their time working on the tarmac at Melbourne's Tullamarine International Airport. Hence the reason for the title of this book.

Obviously, this section is the longest and contains many experiences, and tales from the tarmac. However, such things happen on tarmacs all over the world. This is why the airline industry is so fascinating.

Trucks are an integral part of cargo deliveries and drop-offs at airports around the world. Due to tight security, each truck that enters the inside tarmac area needs to be cleared through the perimeter gates. During 'live' horse or cattle charter deliveries or pick-ups, this can prove a chaotic time for all concerned.

To add to the chaos, many of the trucks were used as shuttles between the holding farm area (quarantine farm) and the airport area where the aircraft was parked. This meant that the drivers of such trucks were generally in a hurry to off-load their cattle, and rush off to get the next load.

One driver had a HUGE bull on his truck that had to be transferred off the truck down a short ramp and into a wooden crate in which the animal was to travel on the aircraft.

"Come on, hurry up ya big oaf!" shouted the driver, and using one of the battery prods touched the bull on the rump to make it rush off his truck. The beast got a fright as the sharp short electric buzz hit its rump! *Clatter clatter thump*! Down the ramp it sped and into the wooden crate. The only problem was that the beast did not pull up in time and thumped into the far end of the crate, effectively 'popping' it out.

Never have so many tarmac workers been seen to scatter so fast! Luckily the bull stopped in its tracks and stood quietly, slightly bewildered, legs spread, with a bemused look at the handler who had gone to it and held it calmly by the ring in its nose whilst the crate was repaired!

Airport refuellers are a breed unto themselves. When working on the tarmac where the 747 freighter was parked out the back of the cargo area, Wendy was often present when they came to fuel the plane. On one occasion, the airline maintenance engineer was busy checking and fixing a bulb in the flight cabin whilst the refueller stood on the platform under the wings. The maintenance engineer had advised the fueller, "I won't be long, fella. Can you just keep an eye on the gauge? I'll be up in the cockpit for a few minutes. I can keep an eye on the level while I'm up in the cabin." Mick then went up into the aircraft, leaving the fueller standing, arms folded and leaning against the platform railing.

Mick was gone longer than expected. He rushed out of the aircraft, ran down the steps and over to the platform, yelling, "Hey mate, stop the fuel!"

The man did nothing, except reply, "I can't! You're the engineer. It's your job to turn this off." By the time Mick got up onto the platform and turned off the fuel line, there was a large pool of excess fuel seeping out onto the tarmac!

The result of this 'incident' was that the airport fire brigade had an un-scheduled 'exercise' of hose practice as they hosed away the excess fuel.

Hey folks, don't get us wrong! Many good friends were made with the refuellers, and on all other occasions, they were great to work with. Guess you could say there are times when the rule book should be ignored. Airline staff certainly don't envy them with their job, a dangerous one at that!

Working for nearly six years for a cargo airline provided many anecdotes for Wendy. The airline employed 'Maintenance Representatives' who were qualified engineers. Each rode with the aircraft on long haul journeys to Australia, Asia or Europe. Wendy admits to feeling pretty safe flying when they were on board, because they wanted to keep that plane in the air!

One particular Maintenance Rep gained quite a reputation in foreign ports for his ingenuity. Wendy's eyes nearly popped one day when she was standing under the wing of the 747 freighter, as Will calmly inspected drops of fuel leaking from the wing tank. "Got any chewing gum, Honey?"

"Chewing gum? No...sorry. But I'll get some from the office. Any particular flavour?"

Will laughed. His tubby tummy bounced up and down over his belt. "It's not for chewing, Honey. I need it to plug the hole! The gum will expand and contract with the heat and cold and will plug the leak perfectly. It will hold until the aircraft is serviced in Hong Kong the other end. There's no time to fix it here."

Later, after a tarmac worker gave Will some fresh gum, Wendy watched fascinated as he put two strips of gum into his mouth. He quietly chewed for five minutes, and then asked a fork lift driver to lift him up to the underside of the wing where the drip of fuel was located. He took the chewing gum from his mouth, rolled it into a nice round ball between his fingers and pressed it firmly over the hole.

Now Wendy and Dave always peer out an aircraft window to see if there are any plugs of 'chewie' on the wing!

747 freighters use a tail strut with lockable wheels to stop the tale tipping onto the ground.

Ground handling agents generally have such tail struts as part of their handling equipment, along with a main deck loader.

Sometimes, the freighters stored a strut in the under belly cargo hold, which could be used in ports without such equipment.

One day, one of the ground crew in another cargo handling agent's area removed a strut from a 747 freighter without permission of the airline ground supervisor.

The tail of the aircraft tipped back onto the tarmac with a loud bang! The nose was now raised up off the ground.

There had been some cargo still positioned in the tail section, making it tail heavy. Luckily the main deck loader for the main side cargo door had not been attached to the aircraft, or more damage would have occurred.

Eventually, the aircraft was re-tilted back onto its front wheels after ground agents hand moved each box from the freight in the tail section, one by one up the sloping floor of the aircraft to the main cargo door, forward of the wings, of the aircraft. One by one, the boxes were handed across the gap to other agents standing on the detached main deck loader.

The aircraft was later towed away to the maintenance sheds, to be checked for any structural damage to the fuselage. It was out of service for days!

Lesson learned? Don't take away a tail strut without permission of the ground supervisor!

Whilst mentioning 'tail heavy', Wendy was involved with another tale of getting a 747 freighter 'heavier' in the tail for the aircraft to be trim for flight.

Wendy had been trained to do a manual load sheet. (This is now a computerised process). She was sometimes given the job when the aircraft was empty, and was being 'ferried' back to Hong Kong from Melbourne, where it then was back in service on the scheduled freighter flights to Los Angeles. The airline didn't have traffic rights from Australia to the USA. The scheduled services came into Australia to Sydney then to Melbourne.

More often than not, the aircraft was chartered by a cargo agent out of Melbourne to overseas ports. These charters were often full of livestock. The other times, the aircraft ferried back to Hong Kong or Taiwan to join the scheduled services to USA.

On this particular day, Wendy was asked if she would like to practice her loading skills on the 747 100 series, which she knew was naturally nose-heavy.

The main problem was that the main deck pallets that were on hand were not heavy enough to be used to put some weight in the tail.

"Hey Wendy, you want something heavy to put on those pallets?" asked one of the porters.

"Yes, I do. Any ideas?"

"Yep, we've seen hundreds of old telephone books in bins, which the airport offices have thrown out, when they got the new ones yesterday. Would they do?"

"Great idea, mate. Can you collect them?"

"Yep!"

Off he went on his tug, with an empty trailer. Half an hour later, he returned with a full trailer of phone books, plus some tie-down nets.

The pallets were loaded with phone books, tie down, and weighed.

"Yes--just what we need to trim the aircraft."

An hour later, the Captain came to the airport, and checked Wendy's load sheet. He grinned at her.

"Well, that's ingenuity!"

Wendy pointed out the porter, who got a big thumbs-up from the Captain. "Great idea, mate!"

The Captain counter signed the load sheet, and made sure that the fuel for the flight was loaded to make the aircraft fly slightly tail heavy. The 747s had the best fuel economy trimmed that way.

After the flight left, Wendy sent off the departure message on the airline's KIAC computer system to Singapore, the destination of the flight, where it had a part-charter of computers destined for Hong Kong.

There was a crew change in Singapore. The aircraft then flew to Hong Kong.

The next morning, Wendy and her Manager had several messages, asking where the paperwork was for the cargo in the back of the aircraft, when it landed in Singapore. There was a similar message from Hong Kong!

Wendy then asked Singapore and Hong Kong to re-read the departure message, which stated clearly, that the two pallets with phone books – 'Old phone books' were there simply as ballast.

Oops! Another problem solved. To this day, Wendy doesn't know what eventually happened to the several hundred old Melbourne phone books.

One night, there was a horse charter ex Melbourne for Taipei. It had been arranged that James would start the loading and Dave would then come on shift at 2am to take over.

When he arrived, the carpark gates were closed. The park was full of horses!

The charterer had taken it upon himself to use the carpark as a corral.

Dave went to him for an explanation.

"What the heck is going on?"

The reply was, "Okay, let me explain. It is Melbourne Cup week, and I have a shortage of horse floats because they are being used to transport horses to Flemington racecourse early this morning."

Dave said, "Well let's get them loaded as quickly as possible. We can't have this mess when my boss comes in at 8am. He'll blow his stack!"

There were still horses in the carpark at 8am. Dave's manager, Tom, on cue, stormed onto the tarmac and gave Dave a mouthful.

Unfortunately, there had been a delay in the loading because the main deck loader had been taken off the aircraft for use on a passenger aircraft in the main terminal. (Passenger aircraft always got priority over cargo aircraft).

The charter flight finally departed Melbourne at 10am, and Dave demanded that the charterer clean up the carpark mess.

Eventually, the day got back to normal operation and everyone's tempers subsided and humour prevailed on hindsight.

The average passenger never realises that cargo aircraft often carry loads of livestock--such as cattle, horses, goats, pigs, alpacas, lamas, and sheep, to name a few--which are generally transported by air to another country for breeding.

Air charter is expensive compared to, for example, cargo ships taking live cattle or sheep destined for slaughter.

One particular charter tarmac tale is about a full load of pregnant cows, headed for Taiwan.

The animals were loaded into large wooden crates which were secured to aircraft pallets with plastic and straw covering the base.

The plastic was used to protect the aircraft mechanisms from corrosive urine. The straw was obviously for the comfort of the cattle.

During the loading of these animals into their crates, there were three cows that went into labour whilst waiting to be loaded.

The vet who was travelling with the aircraft was kept busy. He finally cleared the three new additions to the manifest as fit to travel with their proud mums.

Whilst the birthing took place, there was a frantic rebuild of three pens, where a partition was added to them to help protect the new born calves from being trampled should the plane go through turbulence en-route.

After the aircraft arrived in Taipei, the Melbourne staff received messages that the manifest was incorrect, as there were two extra livestock on board.

It didn't take long to fix the discrepancy, as the vet on board advised that two more calves had been born in flight!

We often wonder if the last two calves born in flight were categorised as citizens of Australia (after their mother) or America (after the Nationality of the aircraft) or Taiwanese (as new immigrants!).

Mail also travels on both passenger and cargo aircraft around Australia and the world.

Once day, there was a whole barrow of mail destined for Israel, which was subject to a full scan by security.

There was a positive 'bleep' recorded on one of the scanners. The bag in question was immediately isolated onto another barrow. The bag had to be opened and the scanner put over each item one by one; a very time consuming job.

It wasn't until security got to the last item that the 'bleep' sounded again.

The envelope was taken to a secure area and very gently sliced open. Inside was aluminium foil wrapped around a large amount of Australian currency. The reason the sender sent it this way was to avoid the contents being picked up by X-ray!

Here was security looking for possible explosives, and instead, they received a payday for government treasury.

Everyone who has travelled by air, whilst waiting in the departure lounge, will have observed ground staff directing in passenger aircraft into the gateways with what looks like two large batons, which are illuminated at night for the Crew to see.

The same procedure occurs with cargo aircraft, coming into the cargo terminal.

One day, Wendy was on the tarmac outside the cargo terminal, standing at the base of a set of engineering steps, which were normally chocked into place, whilst the ground staff ascended the steps to the top to then guide the 747 freighter into the correct position on the tarmac.

Wendy had protective earmuffs on to protect her from the noise of the engines as the huge aircraft approached.

To her bewilderment, the Captain started to weave the aircraft left to right for no apparent reason! The co-pilot was peering at her from the windshield. Wendy looked up to see what the ground staff was doing on the steps.

Shock, horror--the steps were moving backwards down the slight incline of the tarmac, heading toward the hanger behind! Obviously the chocks had not been secured sufficiently.

Wendy immediately raised her hands above her head in a crossed position, which she knew meant STOP!

The crew applied their brakes straight away. In the meantime, several tarmac workers were running to 'rescue' the steps equipment, and the 'guider', who was now very red faced.

Eventually, they pushed the steps back to the correct place and finally, the Captain was able to slightly rev the engines again and taxi the aircraft the last fifty metres to the aircraft chocking area.

When Wendy ascended the stairs to the main door, the maintenance engineer opened the door to greet her.

He giggled and said, "Come on in, Wendy. Golly, we had a good laugh in the flight deck when we realised what was going on. You did the right thing by stopping us! Once we stopped, like you, we just watched the 'Abbot and Costello' show on the tarmac!"

Talking about 'Abbot and Costello' recalls another very funny episode on the tarmac.

Wendy had received a message from her counterpart Jenny, in Sydney, to advise that she had been told by someone in quarantine that 'We think there are some live mice loose on the aircraft heading towards Melbourne. She also advised that Melbourne quarantine had been notified.'

Wendy immediately went outside as the aircraft was due to land. Her Manager was onboard the flight as he was returning from Los Angeles from a course. At this point, Wendy was in charge, as Geoff, her Manager, was her only co-worker. (There were only two Melbourne staff for the airline).

It looked like Ringlings Circus on the tarmac. Quarantine officers were rushing around holding nets. The aircraft taxied in and finally stopped.

The ground engineers hooked up a radio connection to the Captain to explain why the doors had to remain closed, and the crew and Geoff had to remain in the upper deck.

In the meantime, Geoff asked to talk with Wendy. "What the...is going on?"

Wendy then told him that someone in quarantine in Sydney had told Melbourne quarantine that there were mice loose on the aircraft. She also advised Geoff that she had just told Fred, the quarantine officer in charge, that there were laboratory mice manifested on board, and that they were positioned upstairs on one of the seats in the upper deck. This was to ensure that they didn't get frightened, or cold in the main cargo area.

"Geoff, are the mice okay? Is their box secure?"

"Yep! The box is right next to me--all sealed and okay, so what's the problem?"

Wendy handed the microphone across to Fred. He chatted to Geoff for several minutes.

Finally, Fred decided to err on the side of caution, and got his officers to stand on the steps leading up to the main door of the aircraft, holding nets between themselves, to catch any loose mice that might be on board the main deck.

What a comical sight. How on earth any mouse could have been contained by these nets was a wonder in itself.

Ten minutes later, a very red faced Fred descended the stairs, mumbling, "Just wait 'til I find out which clown in Sydney started this rumour in quarantine!" With that comment, Fred and his entourage disappeared off the tarmac.

Geoff finally descended the stairs, holding the large box, containing the expensive laboratory mice.

There was an impromptu applause from all the tarmac workers, followed by laughter.

Snow at Melbourne Airport? Well, let us tell you, such an occurrence is very, very rare! Yes each winter, there is snow on the nearby mountains. The nearest to the airport being Mount Macedon, which is approximately 30 kilometres or 20 miles away, and falls on top of the mount which is a much higher altitude than the area of Tullamarine.

Snow fell one very cold wintery night and Wendy and Dave woke up to find their garden in Sunbury covered in snow. Sunbury normally didn't get snow in winter, and as their home was around 15 kilometres from the airport, they had a dreadful feeling that it was going to be one of those days.

Sure enough, they had to drive very carefully to the airport, passing several cars that had skidded off the country road. The locals were not used to driving in snow!

When they arrived at the cargo terminal, it was chaos on the tarmac. Unlike airports in North America and Europe, Australian airports enjoy basically zero snow during winter.

As a result, there was equipment like snow ploughs or gravel trucks to help make the tarmac and runways safe.

The inbound and outbound aircraft were landing and taking off safely, using reverse engine thrusts to brake.

The tarmac workers were in real strife, as they tried to pull containers full of cargo and passenger baggage around the airport. Wheels spun in the slush, and the container trolleys, being pulled along, were sliding all over the place.

Wendy looked out of her office window, after visiting the tarmac to view the chaos, when, 'splat!' a beautifully executed snowball hit the window in front of her.

A row of grinning faces greeted her from below.

Despite the delays in loading the planes, it had become an almost 'mid-year' Christmas celebration outside. Everyone was having fun in spite of the weather problems.

Eventually, by the afternoon, the temperature rose and the snow had disappeared. Everything returned to normal.

On hind sight, that morning, all the adults working on the tarmac had temporally morphed back to childhood, having fun in the snow!

Melbourne has all sorts of cargo arriving and departing from around the world.

One day, when a freighter was being unloaded outside the cargo terminal, there was a special surprise. The 'Pope Mobile' with its special security bubble came off the aircraft.

Of course, curiosity got the better of the tarmac workers, who wanted to have a closer look at this famous vehicle.

However, to their great disappointment, security would not allow anyone close to the vehicle, except the Vatican Driver who had arrived into Melbourne on the freighter.

When the pallet was rolled off the dolly onto the hoist, it was unlashed and the hoist lowered to ground level so the driver could then drive the Pope Mobile onto the tarmac. He then drove it onto the vehicle transport truck which was parked nearby to the aircraft. The truck then disappeared from sight.

Security followed the truck into Melbourne, ready for the Pope's arrival the next day.

When loading the same freighter for its return to Europe, one of the pallets had a Ferrari saloon car strapped to it.

Naturally, everyone gravitated to the car to have a sticky-beak.

"Hey, look at the mess of that bonnet! Someone has had a smashing time driving this car."

The car had been driven by the son of a prominent businessman in Melbourne. The accident had made headlines in the Melbourne papers a few days earlier.

The car was going back to Italy for a very expensive panel-beat, before being returned to Melbourne.

This emphasised the possibility of huge expenses involved when owning such a car.

One of the most fascinating pieces of equipment used after a livestock charter arrival into Melbourne is called a 'Supersucker'. Wendy's manager, Geoff, sourced it while researching ways to clean out the 747 aircraft, after the pallets containing the livestock were offloaded onto the tarmac, taken out of the crates and loaded into trucks for local transport to the nearby Quarantine station.

Although each pen had heavy plastic covering the base of each crate, with straw for the animal's comfort during flight, there was still debris left behind on board the aircraft.

The 'Supersucker' was simply a huge tanker which parked next to the aircraft. An enormous flexible vacuum hose (approximately one foot in diameter) was attached and moved up into the front of the nose-door of the freighter.

This door opened upwards in the freighter's nose cone via hydraulics, with the end result opening up the fuselage like a large tunnel.

The workers went on board and guided this amazing vacuum cleaner over the floor of the main cargo hold. The loose straw, droppings, and other debris from between the aircraft's roller system was sucked up and sent down to the tanker below on the tarmac, via a large pump on the tanker.

The process was repeated through the lower cargo hold door. Finally, the tanker staff went back through the aircraft with mops and cloths to make sure no urine drops had been left on the floor. Urine is a very corrosive material, and eventually could damage important parts of the aircraft, potentially causing a fatal crash, so this cleaning job was extremely important.

The joke around the airport was that the 'Supersucker' would be perfect for cleaning not only offices or pubs, but maybe a quick clean of homes!

Whilst mentioning 'Supersuckers', passengers will no doubt have noticed smaller tankers attached by flexible hoses to the rear underbelly, when aircraft are standing at the passenger terminals.

These tankers are nicknamed 'Honeycarts' and are pumping out the tanks, holding the waste from the internal toilets on board.

Older generations would remember the 'Honeycarts' coming to the 'outhouses' when emptying septic tanks, in the days before housing estates had mains sewage.

Dave remembers one time when a passenger DC10 arrived into Melbourne from Europe.

At the previous stopover in Singapore, cleaners had rushed through the aircraft, collecting any rubbish and cleaning toilets on board, ready for the next sector to Melbourne.

One of the toilets at the rear of the aircraft had been closed by the air crew, because it was blocked. A cleaner had unblocked this toilet using his broom handle! As a result, the bowl's pipe leading to the main tank had been split.

This resulted in toilet waste from this bowl dripping onto suitcases and the aircraft documents satchel in the bulk hold during the flight from Singapore to Melbourne.

When the bulk hold door was opened at Melbourne, the porters naturally refused to unload the affected bags. However, customs insisted that the documents satchel be taken off the aircraft and documents sorted for customs screening.

The unfortunate cargo clerk, Jack, had the job of sorting these documents using rubber gloves and a mask over his face. He finally presented all the documents to customs.

Eventually the documents came back to the cargo depot to be manifested and distributed to the freight forwarders, messy pong and all!

Needless to say, the duty supervisor sprayed the whole cargo office with a heavily scented deodorant/sanitiser!

The crack in the damaged toilet was fixed in Melbourne and the aircraft continued on to Sydney with the smelly suitcases still on board.

Sydney, being the final destination of the aircraft, meant the cases had to be taken off. The ground crew demanded extra for doing this job. It cost the airline concerned a case of single malt whisky.

Freight is held in large cargo sheds for customs clearance and delivery.

Customs had asked the manager of a particular shed if the new customs dogs could be trained in one of these sheds.

Of course, permission was granted. From that time, it was not unusual to see customs with their dogs-in-training, detecting the smell of drugs and other substances planted in the sheds via a cloth.

The dogs would be commanded to seek, after the trainer had given the smell of a particular scent. They would travel around the sheds, and even were hoisted up onto the top of crates inside the shed.

Very quickly, the dogs would find the scent of what they had been sniffing and tracked the trail to the correct place and then pointed their nose at the cloth.

Their reward was a game of tug of war, or a quick play with a ball, plus heaps of praise.

Wendy and Dave were dog instructors at a local Obedience Club, and were often asked to watch, because the customs people knew that they were dog trainers in their spare time.

Both staff and customers were always fascinated to see these dogs being trained to do such an important job.

Naturally, some passengers at terminals who were trying to smuggle in drugs weren't very happy to see the qualified dogs pointing to their bags!

Wendy was asked if these dogs could do some training on her airline's freighters, whilst they were standing idle during a twelve or twenty-four hour crew rest.

Naturally she gave permission. She was invited to watch one particular new dog, who could actually come down a ladder head first, which is not a normal thing for a dog to do!

The trainer set up a 'drug' cloth in the upper deck of the freighter, where the passenger seats were located. He put the cloth into one of the lockers at the back of the seating area.

Wendy stood and watched, as Snoopy trundled up the retractable ladder, and into the upper deck.

He was concentrating on finding where the hidden 'drug' had been put. Within a few seconds of sniffing around the seats, he ended up at the back bulkhead, then stood up, paws against the bulkhead, nose pointing at the cupboard, where the 'drug' had been hidden.

"Good boy, clever boy!" The handler praised him, and then played a short game of tug-of-war with a piece of rope, much to Snoopy's delight.

"Now watch this clever trick, Wendy. Bet your dogs at Obedience class or Agility classes can't do this!" He then gave another command to Snoopy. "Down you go!"

With that, Snoopy, carefully plodded paw by paw facing nose downwards, and went down the ladder. Normally dogs would have to be carried down such steep steps.

The handler below, picked Snoopy up and cuddled him, and said, "Clever boy!"

The main handler went back down the ladder with Wendy. Once they were all on the tarmac, he said, "You know, Snoopy was a stray and not overly pretty, but we could see that he's intelligent. He's going to be one of our best dogs, especially when we work at the shipping docks. There are lots of ladders to climb there!" With that said, he winked, and they left the tarmac.

Just before the American Cup yacht races in Freemantle, Western Australia, Wendy was on duty when several masts arrived in Melbourne via the freighter.

One of these masts was fifty one feet long. It had been tied down at the side of the main deck freight for its journey from Los Angeles to Melbourne. It had to be off-loaded via the nose door. This was a delicate operation, as the main deck loader was only twenty feet long. There was a long over hang each end. Once the mast had been evenly balanced on the main deck loader, the loader gently moved backwards away from the aircraft nose until it was clear of the nose. The loader then gently lowered the mast to the ground.

It was due to travel the next morning via a semi-trailer truck to Freemantle.

The next day, when the truck was due to arrive to pick up this precious mast for one of the American challengers, there was panic in the cargo shed.

Everyone had seen it the day before on arrival, but no one knew where it was in the cargo shed. Several cargo clerks had searched the shed, to no avail.

Wendy went down stairs from her office to join in the search.

"We can't find it anywhere!"

"Where have you been looking?" asked Wendy.

"All along the sides of the shed. It's a long mast."

Wendy looked around, then looked up into each corner of the shed. Bingo! There it was, standing up in the far corner. It was a huge shed, and obviously the staff on the last shift had put the mast in a safe place, out of the way of hydraulic lifts and forklift trucks which often whizzed down the aisles. It was half hidden by one of the shed's large support girders.

She walked over to the long piece of freight and pointed it out to the cargo handling staff.

"Here it is."

There were several red faces as they manoeuvred the fifty one foot mast out of the shed's corner and onto its side, ready for the semi-trailer when it arrived to collect it for the last leg of the journey to Freemantle.

This mast was part of the American yacht that eventually won the race!

Another tarmac tale about precious cargo involved formula one racing cars.

When Melbourne won the right to hold the Australian Formula One race, six charter 747 aircraft descended on Melbourne airport, full of cars and equipment a week before the big race.

This was a huge operation for Dave's cargo shed and Qantas' shed. Between them, they looked after three freighters each.

The aircraft had to be unloaded immediately, so a large crew of tarmac workers and forklift drivers were on hand to do the work.

Each pallet had a team name on the net. As the pallets were unloaded from the aircraft and un-netted and un-strapped, the fork lift drivers gently took the crated cars off the pallets and took them straight to the waiting trucks. They were then loaded onto the trucks.

When the trucks were full, they left the airport immediately for the Albert Park circuit.

This operation took six hours. When the aircraft were empty and refuelled, they prepared for take-off with new crew to their next destinations.

After the race on the Sunday afternoon, a crew at Albert Park Track started the reverse process. They loaded the trucks, and sent them to the airport. Some went to Dave's terminal, and some to Qantas.

Again, there was a crew of tarmac loaders and forklift drivers to load all the crated cars and equipment back onto the aircraft pallets. Another crew then secured the loads with straps, plastic, and nets, ready for loading onto the freighters when they arrived later that night.

This operation took the tarmac crews well past midnight. When completed, the exhausted men sighed with relief and went home to sleep. All six aircraft departed for the next formula one race destination.

This massive operation went on port after port for the whole Grand Prix season.

A similar operation was used for the 500cc motorbikes and superbikes when they arrived in Melbourne for their races at Phillip Island.

One livestock charter out of Melbourne involved a DC8 aircraft.

The aircraft was to carry live feral goats that had been trucked from the Flinders Rangers region of South Australia.

Whilst these goats were being de-trucked at Melbourne airport, quite a few managed to escape!

Tarmac staff, security, and customs and as many able bodied airport staff as possible were immediately sent to catch these escapees.

In the meantime, the airport runways were closed, because of the danger of livestock being on them when aircraft landed or took off.

Eventually, all the goats were accounted for close to the cargo terminal, and loaded into their pens to await loading onto the aircraft.

There were a few laughs that day, akin to the Keystone Cops as men chased the goats all over the place.

Talk about goats bringing the airport to a standstill!

Back in the 70s, when colour TV first appeared in Australia, a large shipment of colour televisions arrived from Europe. They were due to be collected by truck from the airport after customs clearance. Customs didn't clear this shipment until late afternoon.

The next morning, the airline's cargo handler was 'abuzz' with excitement.

A truck had entered the tarmac through a security gate, telling the clerk that they were collecting the TV shipment. They told the clerk that the paperwork was inside.

Half an hour later, the dozen industrial pallet loads of televisions had been loaded into the covered truck, the load secured, and the driver then left through the same security gate, never to be seen again.

The consignee never received their televisions! From that time onwards, the rule on the tarmac was enforced - 'No paperwork - no freight!'

The 747 freighters can carry twenty and forty foot enclosed containers on board. These containers, of course, are not the heavy ones used for cargo ships, but look very similar.

One day, a heavy shipment of cargo arrived into Melbourne from America.

The shipper's agent had loaded the heavy twenty foot container off the truck and onto the airline's main deck loader in Los Angeles, and it was loaded through the nose of the aircraft.

In Melbourne, however, that same company's Melbourne staff were responsible for taking the container away from the airport.

The airline's cargo handling agent in Melbourne did not have equipment big enough to lift this container off the tarmac and onto the truck.

So, the freight forwarder hired a crane to lift the container. The driver attached the four chains to each corner, ready to lift the load. He was warned by the airline staff and their handling agent of the heavy weight, and asked if it was okay for the container to be lifted that way.

The reply was rather abrupt from the driver. "No problem, mate, this crane will do it easily!"

Famous last words! There was a unanimous gasp as the crane pulled up, and there was a large bang as the top of the container started to neatly peel off at one end, exposing the perishable freight inside.

The poor crane driver couldn't believe it, and yelled, "There's something wrong with this load!"

Rain was also starting to fall, and there was an immediate panic, as the tarmac people went to find tarpaulins to protect the freight from the rain.

Needless to say, the freight was water damaged. The consignee tried to blame the airline, then the cargo handling agent, but as it wasn't their fault, the shipper was entirely at fault. They had loaded the cargo at their store, and instead of distributing the weight evenly inside, they put most of the weight to one end of the container, with wooden planks securing the empty end. This was only obvious after ground staff peered into the opened container whilst doing their damage report. This explained why the roof had peeled back on uplift by the crane.

The airline had used two pallet positions under the container because of its size, and it was loaded in the centre of the aircraft, and had caused no problems on board.

The container also had to be repaired in Melbourne at the shipper's expense.

This reminds us of peeling the lid back off a sardine can, to expose the contents!

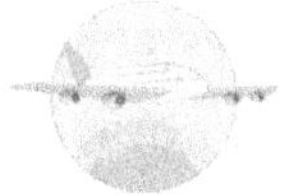

Accidents are bound to happen at airports, but honesty is the best part of valour.

The 747 freighter was parked outside the cargo shed, awaiting the crew who were having a twenty four hour mandatory break.

The aircraft would then fly empty to Hong Kong to reposition back to scheduled services to America.

Wendy's manager had gone out to lunch, and Wendy was sitting doing paperwork in the office when Dave came in and said, "The engineers steps have just hit the side of the aircraft just behind the main side cargo door."

"Any damage?"

"We think so. Can you come and look at it?"

Dave advised Wendy as they went out to the aircraft that one of the tarmac workers had seen the accident happen. There were heavy winds across the tarmac that afternoon, and apparently the chocks on the steps had not held, and the wind literally blew the steps across the apron and into the side of the aircraft. He also added that he had originally been told not to say anything, and that the plane was okay.

He'd ordered that staff member to leave everything as it was, so Wendy, who was the airline's representative on duty, could have a look.

Once they got to the plane, they went up another set of steps to the main cargo door. The first thing that Wendy noticed was that the offending steps had punctured a hole right through the skin of the aircraft!

This meant that the plane possibly could not be pressurised, that there might be damage to the cables and struts beneath the outer skin. A Qantas engineer came to inspect the damage and concurred.

By this time Geoff, Wendy's manager, was back from his lunch break. The crew could not be notified until at the earliest, ten o'clock that evening, which was the end of their uninterrupted break at a Melbourne hotel.

As a result, Geoff gave permission for the Qantas engineers to tow the aircraft down to their maintenance shed to be examined and repaired.

Obviously, that 'ferry' flight due to go out that night was cancelled, and the crew had two extra days R and R in Melbourne.

Passenger and cargo aircraft also carry dangerous goods. These are regulated by rules which specify packaging, compatibility with other dangerous goods, and position of aircraft and in warehouses.

Occasionally there are mishaps. These could be from a wrong declaration by a shipper, bad packaging, or wrong positioning in an aircraft or warehouse. There are also strict procedures to be followed when a dangerous goods incident occurs.

In their time at Melbourne Airport, Dave and Wendy experienced such mishaps.

One such incident occurred at Melbourne airport one day, which resulted in the whole bond store being evacuated and the airport fire brigade being called.

A forty-four gallon drum of a black thick liquid had fallen off a barrow and split open. The liquid was oozing onto the floor.

The airway bill had not specified the exact description of this liquid. The fire brigade attended to isolate this cargo, identify it and to eventually clean it up. Obviously the clean-up bill was going to the shipper.

It turned out that this liquid was a black wax, which was the base for sliced cheese! Colouring and flavouring was to be added to this wax in the destination port.

Needless the say, most people involved went right off the plastic covered, sliced cheese that was made out of this recipe!

Another incident on the same tarmac, involved a large delicate piece of machinery that had arrived from the USA.

The machine had been successfully offloaded from the 747 freighter and put onto a dolly and then towed into the warehouse, for the consignee's truck to collect after the paperwork had cleared customs.

Wendy happened to be present in the warehouse, checking some inbound stores for her airline which had been on the same flight.

She looked at the huge shrink-wrapped machine, which was now sitting on the ground on its wooden pallet.

The warehouse crew were asked by the consignee's driver to lift the machine up and onto the truck.

It had been drizzling with rain outside on the tarmac, and the plastic glistened in the afternoon sun as the fork lift manoeuvred itself to lift the heavy load.

The load was finally lifted, but as it neared the edge of the truck, the whole machine suddenly toppled over and fell to the concrete floor with a loud *Bang!*

The was a moment of absolute silence, then chaos broke loose, as the truck driver and the fork lift driver started to shout at each other.

The consignee, who had also witnessed the accident, also joined in the verbal fray.

Eventually, the load was righted, but unfortunately there was some obvious external damage to the machine. Wendy also wondered to herself what else had been damaged internally.

A damage form was filled out, and the consignee sent it to Wendy's airline, claiming for damages.

The end result was that the actual machine was found to be 'top heavy' and this was not declared on the freight nor the airway bill.

The freight itself had been safe in the aircraft as it had been netted and strapped down onto the aircraft's pallet.

Once the netting and straps had been removed, the top heavy machine was in immediate danger of toppling over if moved. The damp conditions outside had not helped.

The claim was therefore refused by the airline, so the consignee then made a claim on the ground handling agent. The ground handling agent also refused the claim, as the engine had not been declared or labelled as 'top heavy'.

One lesson learnt - be very wary of top heavy freight shipments in the future, by all companies concerned!

One day, cargo off a passenger aircraft was driven into Dave's company's warehouse to be checked off against the paperwork.

An aircraft pallet of general cargo was un-netted and the plastic taken off. Suddenly, a cat jumped out from amongst the cargo!

Panic! "Close all doors! That cat must not escape."

Animal Quarantine was immediately notified and all staff requested to leave the warehouse.

Quarantine arrived with their usual nets. It was their job to catch the wayward cat and to take it away.

The aircraft had come from Bangkok, and the fear was that the cat had accidentally hitched a ride to Australia. Animals coming in from Asia or overseas all need to have correct health papers, vaccinations and import permits, in order to protect the Australian animal population.

It took over an hour for the cat to be caught by Quarantine. Their staff all wore very thick gloves but still, a Quarantine officer was scratched on the arm. He was immediately rushed to hospital for a tetanus injection and check-up.

Finally the cat was taken away, and humanely euthanized. This cat was obviously a Bangkok Airport stray, and therefore could have been a rabies carrier.

In 1983, Wendy drove her second-hand car to work at the airport.

As she drove into her airline's handling agent's carpark, she noticed that the temperature gauge was suddenly rocketing sky high.

It couldn't have happened at a worse time, as the car had already been allocated as a 'trade-in' for her new car. She was going to exchange cars that afternoon!

Panic buttons were pressed mentally in Wendy's brain. What could she do? Steam was coming out of the bonnet. Fortunately, the car was parked before she noticed the temperature gauge. With the engine turned off, she got out of the car.

A friendly face smiled at her. It was a Qantas engineer who she knew who had worked on her airline's aircraft when maintenance was needed. He had been walking past on his way to work at Qantas, next door.

"Looks like you have a leaking radiator, Wendy."

"I just hope that the car's head hasn't blown," replied Wendy. (Yes, Wendy's father had taught her basic car knowledge years earlier).

"Okay, let's have a look."

Wendy then told him about her dilemma of the trade-in.

Five minutes later, the engineer smiled at her. "Don't panic, the engine head's fine - and I have a can of 'magic' fluid which I'll pour into the radiator which will stop the leak, so you can safely drive this down to Essendon and trade it in for your new car."

What a relief! When Wendy finished work, she drove her car to the sales yard and handed in the keys. Her new car was waiting for her.

There was never any feedback or complaint that her car wasn't fully 'fit'. Wendy presumes that the special 'aviation' stop leak fluid did more than a patch up job on the car.

Such was the friendliness of the 'opposition' airline personnel in those days at Tullamarine.

Tullamarine airport is located on a huge, flat open country plain, north of Melbourne. As a result there can be very heavy winds.

One such day, the wind was gale force and the ground staff were asked to tie down any loose equipment on the tarmac. Unfortunately this order was too late.

Aircraft flat pallets were being blown across the tarmac and one even took off over a fence and dropped on top of some staff cars, causing quite considerable damage.

Some big empty freighter containers in the equipment yard started to move. One porter thought he was being clever, so he drove his tug and parked inside the container. The container still started to move on the tarmac, so the driver quickly jumped out of the way.

Such was the strength of the wind that day. Luckily no one was hurt, but quite a number of aircraft pallets and containers were badly damaged, and insurance claims had to be made by the airlines. Insurance claims were also made by the car owners.

Another tarmac 'wind' experience happened when Wendy's airline freighter was taxiing into the chocks area outside the cargo shed.

This time, however, the damage was caused by wind created by the engines, commonly known as exhaust wind.

The batons man was guiding in the aircraft, and made the crew turn slightly to the right as it approached the terminal.

Unfortunately, some of the manmade cattle pens were located rather far out on the tarmac. These pens had been made by ground staff the night before, ready for a charter flight. The inbound aircraft that had blown the crates was operating the charter outbound the next day, after crew rest. It had started to blow away some of its charter equipment!

Whoosh! Away flew a couple of the crates across the tarmac as they copped the full blast of the number one engine. Ground staff standing nearby the crates ran for cover.

The batons man instantly stopped the aircraft, and the crew impatiently waited while the ground staff retrieved the crates, and moved them closer to the terminal.

The captain wasn't exactly impressed, as fuel was needlessly used up whilst standing still on the tarmac.

Five minutes later, the still idling aircraft was again able to move forward, and stop on the chocks one hundred yards further down the tarmac.

One big lesson was learnt that day--do not put the wooden cattle crates so far out on the tarmac when there is a 747 freighter coming into the cargo area!

A full load of cattle was due to fly out of Melbourne to Taipei late one night.

Wendy had been on duty from 9am to 5pm, and was due to hand over charter duties to another staff member from Sydney, who was covering the Melbourne manager, who was on leave.

Unfortunately, not long after that staff member arrived on the inbound freighter, she became ill.

Wendy then had to stay on duty until the charter flight had left the next morning. There was no one else to cover her position!

In the meantime, the crew on the inbound flight from Sydney needed their twelve hour break.

Wendy was left alone in the office whilst the Sydney staffer went to the airport hotel under a doctor's order.

The handling agent's staff got food for Wendy. Dave, who was on duty at that time, was due back at 2am to take over from the first charter shift.

What a disastrous start it was to that charter! By the time Wendy had phoned the crew twelve hours after they had rested, the flight had already been rescheduled to depart four hours later at 7am.

In the meantime, the handling agent supervisor had been supervising the loading of cattle into the pens, ready for loading onto the aircraft.

By 2am, Dave had returned to the airport to take over as supervisor on the tarmac, after an eight hour break.

The loading was slow and eventually there were no tarmac staff left to continue the loading, as they had to return a few hours later for their own shifts.

The main deck had been fully loaded, but the nine pens for the belly were still on dollys on the tarmac, next to the aircraft.

Wendy also now faced the problem of the crew who were ready to fly the charter, might get close to going out of hours again, as the flight departure was now further delayed. The flight time was eight hours, and the crew realised too, that the aircraft needed to be loaded at the latest by 6.30am.

Finally, a few of the ground staff had returned to help finish the loading. Dave had to help load as well as supervise.

Dave was on the tarmac. One of the pallets locks had jammed, and he tried to release it by hand. At the same time, the cattle moved in the pen and the crate moved and jammed his fingers!

He immediately went into the office for first aid, leaving the rest of the crew to finish the loading.

Wendy was waiting in the office for the crew to come through to the aircraft. She had been over to the main passenger terminal to collect the weather reports and flight plans for the Captain.

The crew saw Dave with his hand bandaged, and holding it in the air. Naturally they asked what had happened, as they knew him as Wendy's husband.

Finally, the aircraft was ready to depart, and Wendy went out on the tarmac again with Dave in tow, holding his hand in the air.

The airline maintenance engineer who was travelling on the flight came down the aircraft steps, with one hand in the air, and a finger under his nose, doing the goose step!

Wendy suddenly realised that he was trying to make Dave laugh at his injury. He succeeded! Everyone had a good laugh. He then gave Wendy a quick hug and said, "The Captain is putting in a special report about you; working without a rest for twenty four hours! Really above and beyond the call of duty we reckon, gal!" He turned to Dave and added, "Get to your doctor as soon as possible mate. That finger needs proper medical attention."

With those words, he went back up the stairs and the main cargo door was closed.

It was over half an hour after the flight had finally departed that Wendy was able to finish all the departure messages for the airline's home base in Los Angeles, and to Taipei, the aircraft's destination.

Wendy then had to drive Dave to their doctor's surgery, where he had his finger attended to. They both finally crashed into bed at 9.30am, utterly exhausted, but proud that not only the ground team had helped, but the airline crew had also been on hand to get the flight out.

They realised that not only did they have a happy marriage, but had also worked like a real team together on the tarmac through such a difficult time.

That's all part of working on a tarmac, and is just one of many 'Tarmac Tales'.

Postscript

Names have been changed to maintain anonymity, with the exception of course, ourselves, as Wendy and Dave, when relating some of our experiences. None of the Tarmac Tales are intended to hurt anyone; merely to help all people who travel, or work in the industry, have a good giggle, and a better understanding at what can happen behind the scenes!

We've both left the airline industry years ago, when the 747 aircraft were the international workhorses of the air. Amazingly enough, the 747s are still the main cargo workhorses of the air.

Since that time, we've experienced many of the new passenger aircraft and airlines--recently the Airbus A380--a truly magnificent piece of engineering!

You can find ALL our books up at on our website at:

http://www.writers-exchange.com

All Wendy's books:

http://www.writers-exchange.com/Wendy-Laing/

All our funny fiction:

https://www.writers-exchange.com/category/genres/comedy-humour/

About the Author

Wendy **Laing** is one half of the pseudonym or pen name "Dalziel Laing" of Dianne Dalziel and Wendy Laing, the co-authors of *Mirror, Mirror.* She is also a multi-published author in her own right.

In retirement, a writer, with a Teaching Diploma, a Bachelor of Arts Degree with majors in professional Writing (creative writing editing, publishing and Journalism) and Communications (mass media, and gender imaging) with electives in Literary Studies and Sociology, and Master of Arts (project/thesis called: "Severance Packages, A crime/Paranormal Novel and Exegesis focussing on the electronic and Digital publication of Creative Writing".

A "Jill-Of-All-Trades" Teacher, curriculum consultant, travel consultant, International Airline employee in passenger and cargo areas at Melbourne International Airport and city offices, and a Professional Dog

Trainer! Wendy's had articles published in *The Sunbury Times* and *The Anthony Warlow International Newsletter*.

Member of the FAW (Fellowship of Australian Writers)
Member of the VWC (Victorian Writers Centre)
Lifetime Alumni of Victoria University
Member of Sister in Crime

Widowed in 2016, Wendy lives in a retirement village with her four pawed family, Vicky, a sooky & loving adopted black Greyhound, whom she has trained and takes to Pet therapy at the local aged care each week - a hobby that she has enjoyed for over 30 years.

Keep track of Wendy's many books on her author page:
http://www.writers-exchange.com/Wendy-Laing/

If you enjoyed this author's book, then please place a review up at the site of purchase, and any social media sites you frequent!

If you want to read more about books by this author, they are listed on the following pages...

Captain Angus, the Lighthouse Ghost

{Mid-Grade Reader: Paranormal}

Two children holidaying at the Cape Otway Lighthouse Station in Victoria Australia meet the ghost of an old Scottish sea captain who roams the world helping the 'spirits' of lighthouses and helping 'conserve' the towers. Captain Angus befriends the children and takes them on virtual reality trips via a magic time tunnel. Together, they experience sailing on an old sailor's vessel, see a shipwreck rescue, witness the tower being built, and even meet one of their own ancestors!

Publisher: http://www.writers-exchange.com/Captain-Angus-the-Lighthouse-Ghost/

Cock of the Walk

{Murder Mystery}

When Sir Peter Percival, owner of the Woodburne Wine Estate and former member of Parliament, is found dead, three Australian detectives embark on a baffling investigation in which it appears *everyone* has a motive...

Publisher: http://www.writers-exchange.com/Cock-of-the-Walk/

Jane Doe Mystery Series

{Mystery/Paranormal}

As the daughter of a policeman who died in the line of duty, Inspector Jane Doe, head of Melbourne Homicide, is single-mindedly driven to seek justice for all. But Jane is no ordinary detective. She can communicate with the ghosts of murder victims. Not wanting to be dismissed as mentally unstable, she must keep her secret from all but her husband and her senior officer, using each victim's information to subtly direct her team in the right direction on each case. Jane realizes she's the only thing standing between a killer being brought to justice and a monster getting off scot-free. But, with each case she solves, her fear that the police hierarchy will accidentally discover her secret forces her to walk a fine line indeed.

Book 1: Flowers from the Grave

Recovering from near fatal head injuries received from a serial killer, who is still at large, Inspector Jane Doe, head of Melbourne Homicide, is staying in an isolated clifftop cottage. Ryan, a stranger on the beach, befriends her. But Jane's idyllic sojourn turns into a nightmare. Flowers arrive with threatening notes attached. Worse, she can't help but believe that Ryan is some kind of ghost, and, if he is, is he friend or foe? Has the serial killer she apprehended in the name of justice returned to finish what he started and make her his next victim?

Publisher: http://www.writers-exchange.com/Flowers-From-The-Grave/

Book 2: Severance Packages

Set in the peaceful town of Sunbury, Australia, Inspector Jane Doe, head of Melbourne Homicide, once again deals with a serial killer after grisly, dismembered body parts are discovered at a local winery and the rubbish dump. Jane has to act fast to stop any more of these 'severance packages' from being delivered.

Publisher: http://www.writers-exchange.com/Severance-Packages/

Book 3: Haunted Heart

Head of Melbourne Homicide, Inspector Jane Doe's first Cold Case involves the recent death of a daughter of a Member of Parliament. After he disagrees with the first coroner's verdict of accidental death, the MP secures a second autopsy that reveals his daughter was murdered. At the same time, Jane's husband Oliver is dealing with a young heart transplant recipient who's having nightmares of being murdered. Elsewhere, another law enforcement officer, Steve Ho, investigates the murder of an eminent heart transplant surgeon found in a local lake. Jane, Oliver and Steve become embroiled in a case that will surely haunt them all for years to come.

Publisher: http://www.writers-exchange.com/Haunted-Heart/

Book 4: Cadavers' Cave

Chief Superintendent of the Cold Case Squad, Jane Doe has a formidable list of special, unsolved cases littering her desk. Taking a break is a luxury she doesn't often allow herself. However, during a rare weekend off, she catches a news story involving a dead body wrapped in a plastic shroud. The gruesome discovery was made in the cliffs below the Point Lonsdale Lighthouse--directly near the entrance to the Port Phillip Bay in Victoria, Australia. Rough winter weather combined with unusually heavy, high tides washed away the grave, leaving it partially covered in rocks and seaweed. The coroner estimates that the body had been buried there for at least a year. The last thing Jane needs is another case to hit her already

groaning desk, but something eerie took place in Cadavers' Cave and she may be the only one who can solve a mystery equally troubling and tragic.
Publisher: http://www.writers-exchange.com/Cadavers-Cave/

Book 5: The Ghostly Gum

Detective Chief Superintendent Jane Doe has a formidable list of cold cases on her desk. This latest one involves an unidentified person, murdered seventeen years earlier.

It is not only a perplexing case, but also an exploratory challenge for all involved as the squad try not only to identify the victim, but sort out suspects who are involved in money laundering, drugs and family feuds.

Jane's team are challenged to find solid forensic proof to use against the main suspect, so he doesn't get away with a cold-blooded murder.
Publisher: http://www.writers-exchange.com/The-Ghostly-Gum/

Mind's Eye-The imagery of remembered scenes

{Poetry}

A collection of poems encompassing one life filled with images from childhood, family, pets, the Australian countryside around, and delivered with a touch of homespun philosophy.

Publisher: http://www.writers-exchange.com/Minds-Eye/

Sir Henry, the Knight in Space

{Science Fiction/Mid-Grade Reader}

Twin boys accidentally beam the ghost of 14th century Sir Henry de Bohun into their father's spaceship in 3000 AD. Let the fun begin as they take a virtual trip back in time to visit Sir Henry's English castle!

Publisher: http://www.writers-exchange.com/Sir-Henry-the-Knight-In-Space/

Mirror, Mirror
with Di Dalziel (writing as Dalziel Laing)
{Murder Mystery}

Inspector Georgina Borg's life is an emotional rollercoaster. She's deeply in love with Professor Richard Thompson yet can't get herself to commit to a permanent relationship--a puzzle even she can't explain adequately. At work, she's in charge of a case pursuing a serial killer who's remained a mystery for ten long years. She's followed his distinctive but maddeningly elusive trail from Sydney to Melbourne. Now suddenly the killer targets a victim with an entirely new profile. Despite the change in modus operandi, Borg is certain it's the same killer. Just when she thinks she's close to solving the puzzle and revealing his identity at last, her should-be, would-be fiancé becomes the prime suspect!

Publisher: http://www.writers-exchange.com/Mirror-Mirror/

Tarmac Tales
By Wendy and Dave Laing

In this fact-based collection of experiences in the airline and travel industries gathered by authors with a combined fifty-two years working in all capacities of the business, you'll be given a behind-the-scenes look at the inner operations of this sometimes funny, sometimes sad, but always entertaining trade.

Publisher: http://www.writers-exchange.com/Tarmac-Tales/

Under the Coolabah Tree

{A Collection of Australian Poetry}

Fun, amusing, sometimes rowdy and always delightfully full of Australian colour, this collection of Australian Bush poems is best read out loud--if you dare to try an Aussie accent!

Publisher: http://www.writers-exchange.com/Under-the-Coolabah-Tree/

If you want to read more about other Humorous novels by this publisher, they are listed on the following pages...

Can You Smell Burning?
By Karen Fainges

{Humour}

Ever had one of those days when your car is nearly totalled by a flying cow and the only clothing you can find during a house fire is an old robe that doesn't close in front? Well, misery loves company, so join Karen Fainges as she journeys through some of the moments in her life that didn't seem quite as funny at the time. Contained in this book are the stories of a family that lives in interesting times.

Publisher: http://www.writers-exchange.com/Can-You-Smell-Burning/

Laugh Out Louds For Moms
By Robin Helene Vogel

Dedicated to mothers everywhere, readers will laugh out loud as they read familiar little poems and brief anecdotes about the pitfalls, pratfalls, joys and horror stories associated with being a mother. Pregnancy cravings, projectile vomiting, post-birth and permanent weight gain, pediatrician's visits, despising your kid's choice of mate--all the predicaments are included to amusingly affirm to readers they're not alone in the insane asylum motherhood can so often be. Rest assured that others are also sitting in playpens in fetal positions sucking their thumbs!

Publisher: http://www.writers-exchange.com/Laugh-Out-Louds-For-Moms/

My Mommy is Insane
By Koni Coward

Mommy's frazzled nerves are humorously illustrated in this original poem. Mothers of small children can identify with this book just as children who love to drive their mothers crazy will want to linger on every single page of mischief.

Publisher: http://www.writers-exchange.com/My-Mommy-Is-Insane/

Uncle Billy's Chicken Hut and Salvation Emporium
By Jeffrey G. Roberts

You know you're dead but not quite sure how it happened or where to go?

Come on in! Uncle Billy'll steer you right!

West of Phoenix, you'll discover a place as alien as Mars sitting in paranormal obscurity and trans-dimensional anonymity. Part diner, part carnival, you can't get there by car, plane or even horseback. You won't find it on a map or stumble upon it. Well, unless you're dead...

Welcome to Uncle Billy's Chicken Hut & Salvation Emporium. Who is Uncle Billy and how did he get the ability to ease the passing of muddled souls? Who knows? Suffice it to say he's been here for centuries. The only threat to his job of transitioning the dearly departed to the appropriate afterlife are interdimensional pests...and they've infested the Emporium. Getting rid of them'll take some doing, but, in the meantime, set a spell. Not like you're going anywhere, right?

Publisher: http://www.writers-exchange.com/Uncle-Billys-Chicken-Hut/

You can find ALL our books up on our website at:

http://www.writers-exchange.com

All Wendy's books:

http://www.writers-exchange.com/Wendy-Laing/

All our funny fiction:

https://www.writers-exchange.com/category/genres/comedy-humour/

www.ingramcontent.com/pod-product-compliance
Lightning Source LLC
Chambersburg PA
CBHW071321130726
47996CB00002B/573